STATES OF
DENIAL

DEDICATION

This book is dedicated to the memory of Betty Meyler, who was a great friend and an avid student of all things paranormal. Her presence will be with us always.

It is also dedicated to the memory of Ken Potts, who provided the authors with up-to-the-minute data on strange phenomena from around the world. We will greatly miss his wit and banter.

STATES OF DENIAL

THE TUSKAR ROCK INCIDENT AND OTHER MYSTERIES

CARL NALLY
DERMOT BUTLER

FOREWORD BY ÉAMONN ANSBRO, FRAS
DIRECTOR, KINGSLAND OBSERVATORY

MERCIER PRESS
IRISH PUBLISHER – IRISH STORY

MERCIER PRESS

Cork

www.mercierpress.ie

© Carl Nally and Dermot Butler, 2013

© Foreword: Éamonn Ansbro, 2013

ISBN: 978 1 78117 147 9

10 9 8 7 6 5 4 3 2 1

A CIP record for this title is available from the British Library

Printed and bound in the EU.

CONTENTS

ACKNOWLEDGEMENTS

We wish to acknowledge and thank the following people for their encouragement and support in the research and writing of this book: Carlo Cretaro, Amy Nally, Val Young, Gerry Butler, Fiona Loughran, Ross Nally, Graham Meates, Kevin Jenkinson, B. J. O'Brien, John Scarry, A. J. Gevaerd, Maureen O'Toole, Rob Gahan and Mike Foylan.

We would especially like to thank Éamonn Ansbro, astronomer and director of Kingsland Observatory near Boyle, County Roscommon. In 1975 he detected moonquakes which were verified by NASA, and in 1976 he discovered a nova, *Vulpecula*. In more recent times, he has contributed to NASA's 'Deep Impact' mission and is leading the way towards a scientific comprehension of the perplexing riddle posed by Unidentified Aerial Phenomena. His involvement in and papers on the subject are outstanding. We are grateful to him for his contribution and friendship.

We are indebted to all those who have contacted us about their personal experiences, and who gave freely of their time to be interviewed and to complete the necessary paperwork which ensured the inclusion of their experiences in our files.

Finally, we wish to express our gratitude to the many contributors who had faith in us to help them explore their paranormal encounters and to bring their experiences together as one, with one understanding.

FOREWORD

Two months before Orville and Wilbur Wright's historic flight at Kitty Hawk, North Carolina, USA, a top scientist declared that 'no possible combination of known substances, known forces of machinery and known forms of force can be united in a practical [flying] machine'. Germ theory was first advanced in ancient Sanskrit texts thousands of years ago, but wasn't widely accepted until late in the nineteenth century. The British Astronomer Royal declared space travel 'utter bilge' in 1956, one of a long line of scientists who 'proved' it was impossible.

Throughout history, it has been difficult, even impossible, to promote the acceptance of new discoveries. Yet during the last two centuries there has been a veritable explosion of new cures, theories, techniques and inventions that have revolutionised aviation, space travel, communications, medicine and warfare.

Most of them, of course, were deemed 'impossible'.

This book presents an intriguing look at Unidentified Aerial Phenomena (UAP) and other mysteries. The literature on UAP is littered with examples of people making their minds up without studying the evidence. Even worse is when they do study the evidence and then reject certain aspects of that evidence that do not fall in line with their preconceived positions.

Many scientific misjudgements have been made in the past, as well as occasional resistance towards accepting the veracity (or lack of it) of observed scientific/physical phenomena. The authors of this book, two well-known Irish researchers of the paranormal, argue that the same problems apply to the topics discussed here.

The writing style is lively, friendly, engaging, packed with fascinating information and quite accessible. I found it captivating. This book can be enjoyed by anyone, no matter what their beliefs are about the mysteries discussed. This includes science buffs and anybody with common sense who is interested, in particular, in how the situation concerning UAP and other mysteries can be suppressed (or ignored, or disbelieved) until the evidence becomes overwhelming.

After more than sixty years of denial, ridicule and dismissal, many scientists, academics, political figures and senior military personnel are taking these topics seriously. For those who question why, this book provides the answer. The authors offer compelling accounts that physical objects, with flight characteristics not yet achievable through known technology, are active in many mysterious events in our skies. They also investigate other fascinating subjects that need to be solved.

Throughout the book, the authors present irrefutable evidence that UAP – which are seemingly able to manoeuvre in ways that defy the laws of physics – actually exist.

UAP and other mysteries seem like tangible, mocking proof that the universe is a much stranger place than humanity, with its dogmatic 'consensus reality', wants to accept.

There are millions of people around the world who have had strange experiences that no one can yet explain, because such experiences, such phenomena, defy explanation by the rules of physics that we take for granted. This book details these experiences and phenomena, despite the media, scientific and governmental states of denial.

Éamonn Ansbro,
Astronomer
Director, Kingsland Observatory

INTRODUCTION

This book's pages tell of mysterious events in aviation, after which the details of the experiences of those involved have either been tailored to meet the demands of officialdom, or simply ignored because they are deemed to be unacceptable to the reporting norms of the aviation safety and regulatory authorities.

Our research shows that the sky above us can be a very peculiar place. In attempting to investigate various mysteries of the sky, some researchers have run the gauntlet of having their careers adversely affected. A few, though, have been determined enough to carry on with their research work, come what may. Astronomer Éamonn Ansbro, who wrote this book's foreword, is one such individual.

Those who involve themselves in the study of unidentified aerial phenomena (UAP) routinely suffer the slings and arrows of either less open-minded contemporaries, or a debunking (though rarely informed) media corps. Or both. A thick skin is called for in such dealings. However, when suspected elements of the intelligence services become involved, surely even the most ardent sceptic is forced to face the fact that there *is* something to the subject after all, despite any comments to the contrary from the political masters of such elements. Meeting a wall of silence from the world of officialdom about UAP is one thing, but it is quite another when unknown forces engage in breaking into researchers' homes, when nothing at all is stolen but their investigative work has clearly been rifled through. We live in a shadowy world where nothing really changes as governments come and go, but where a lid is still kept on certain subjects thanks to an 'old guard' of senior career civil servants. The UAP puzzle is one such subject, with awkward questions being routinely parried or ignored. Or else they are buried, sometimes for years, or decades, thanks to an efficient secrecy policy, or managed data (or even no data at all) being released to the press. It is through such policies that certain uncomfortable events are buried well away from public scrutiny.

The political realm is a world where phone taps have been put in place quite routinely and where odd things tend to happen when certain lines of enquiry are pursued. Unusual goings-on with telephone lines were suspected as long ago as during the course of the first official Tuskar Rock investigation in Ireland – involving the Irish government's own investigator. In more recent years the Irish government has also allegedly been involved in eavesdropping on environmentalists campaigning against the building of an oil pipeline on the Atlantic coast.

Concrete evidence of covert activity came to light as two determined researchers tried to look into how a UAP sighting had triggered a security alert at the country home of the UK's Home Secretary in 1997. The alert was officially denied, of course, but the investigators were left with firm evidence of an attempt having been made to monitor their work on the case.

It is the secrecy surrounding the subject of UAP, a secrecy perpetrated by powerful government agencies, that is keeping the populace in ignorance of the truth. These phenomena are so perplexing that they are beyond our current understanding. Either the world's governments are equally mystified by the conundrums posed by these phenomena, or they are deliberately and systematically hiding the reality of the subject from their citizens.

One way or the other, their official approach continues to be a state of denial.

1

THE SHORT ARM
OF THE LAW

When unidentified aerial phenomena are seen and reported in the press, an ever-sceptical public focuses its attention not on what was actually observed, but on the credibility of the eyewitnesses who make the reports. This attitude is nurtured by the reporting style of much of the printed and broadcast media. Almost without fail, a journalist's wording in their UAP coverage, spoken or written with tongue firmly in cheek, plays up the image of the witness claiming to have seen either little green men or a craft straight out of the TV series *Star Trek*. Couple this style of reporting with such reproduced images as that of a toy alien bought from a novelty store, and very quickly the report that hits the airwaves or newsstands bears little if any resemblance to what *really* happened. The 'truth' thus becomes what the reporters (or their editors) think it *should* be.

In our previous book, *Conspiracy of Silence* (Mercier Press, 2006), we mentioned this aspect of the media and public perception of UAP. Several years later, little has changed. It is still our experience that much of the public's media-driven perception of these phenomena is that they and visiting extraterrestrial (ET) spacecraft are deemed to be one and the same. Any person claiming to have seen a structured airborne 'object', which constitutes just one aspect of UAP – and thus, as much of the press would have us believe, an alleged vehicle from some other planet – is pigeon-holed as being mentally unhinged. Both assertions are untrue: the 'U' in the 'UAP' acronym stands only for 'unidentified', while witnesses coming forward have included such people as professional astronomers, law enforcement personnel, military and commercial pilots, etc.

As far as pilots are concerned, some of the commercial aviators we dealt with while researching our previous book, and who reported unusual incidents to us, are still deemed to be perfectly fit to fly many hundreds of people around the world every week. If such pilots are mentally well enough to fly, despite having seen things in the sky that they couldn't explain, then they serve as a useful yardstick by which to judge the reliability of UAP reports. The sceptics will point out that even highly trained pilots can make mistakes, as they are only human. This may be true in some pilot sightings, but there are very often other airborne witnesses to the same events, and sometimes even radar detection of the aerial anomalies to corroborate what has been reported.

The bottom line is that, in researching anomalous aerial phenomena, there needs to be a yardstick, a benchmark by which the dependability of the claims of witnesses can be judged. If highly trained pilots are considered believable, it is only logical that the testimonies of at least some witnesses on the ground, the claims of ordinary members of the public, also deserve careful consideration.

The men and women who fly us around the globe for business and pleasure, and the military aircrew who serve at home and abroad, are not the only people who spend their working lives in our skies. Neither are they the only people into whose hands we place our trust – or our lives. The world of law enforcement has its own highly skilled and well-trained personnel, people who are accustomed to both daytime and night-time flying and observation, and who can surely be expected to know the difference between the planet Venus, swamp gas, or something more exotic in the sky. In several cases in quite recent years, pilots and observers in police helicopters have become startled witnesses to nearby unexplained aerial activity.

A SCARE IN WALES

In the early summer of 2008, a helicopter being operated by the South Wales Police came too close for comfort to an unidentified aerial vehicle. The aircraft was hovering at 500 feet (around 152 metres), preparing to land at the Royal Air Force (RAF) base at St Athan, near Cardiff. Suddenly, the three crew members saw what they described as a 'flying saucer-shaped object', darting towards their aircraft from below.

The pilot banked sharply, very possibly preventing a collision, and turned his helicopter to pursue the craft. He continued on a course out over the Bristol Channel and towards the North Devon coast, but the unidentified craft easily outpaced the helicopter, which was running low on fuel. The police gave up the pursuit.

The incident occurred in the early hours of 8 June, with the Irish edition of *The Sun* newspaper publishing its account almost two weeks later, on 20 June. Journalist John Coles wrote a report that used quotes from an unnamed source. However, his account was sombre – despite the *'Ello, 'Ello, UFO!* caption – and it raised serious questions concerning both aircraft safety and air defence issues.

Coles reported that the UK's Ministry of Defence (MoD) commented that it didn't know anything about the incident. This was despite the fact that it had reputedly occurred, initially, at or very close to a defence installation and at 500 feet (152 metres). Still, the MoD did state that it was 'not advisable for police helicopters to go chasing what they think are UFOs'.[1] This was curious, as the MoD had for many years followed the official line that such reported objects were of 'no defence significance'. If these objects are known in some way to be harmless, then one must wonder why the police aircraft should not have followed it. (Incidentally, one will notice how, to play down the seriousness of such material and thus invite much of the press to attack it further, even government sources continue to include the term 'UFO' in official releases. The use of this term has largely gone the way of the 1940s–50s 'flying saucer' terminology, as far as inducing ridicule and 'the giggle factor' are concerned. In using the term UAP in this book, we incorporate more than just reported aerial objects or craft, as the following chapters will show.)

While the MoD said it had no knowledge of the incident, Coles still included in his report a comment from a spokesperson for the South Wales Police, who said that they 'can confirm the Air Support Unit sighted an unusual aircraft', and that the episode 'was reported to the relevant authorities for their investigation'.[2]

The reporting of the incident was not limited to the popular tabloids. These 'red tops' – so-called because of their distinctively coloured mastheads – have garnered a reputation over the decades for sensationalism, but this story also appeared on 20 June in the *Daily Telegraph* newspaper. The next day, 21 June, it appeared as far away as in the Pune edition of *The Times of India*. It repeated the words of the South Wales Police official and then went on to describe some other intriguing sightings, reports of which had recently been disclosed in previously secret files held by the MoD.

Among these files were 'official reports' of sightings by police officers and senior airport personnel. Recorded on official forms, the reports were compiled by the MoD between 1978 and 2002, with a further 150 files scheduled to be made public by 2012. One of the released files detailed how a Sea King helicopter crew tracked two unknown objects on their radar system for 40 miles in September

1985. The objects travelled at a rate of nearly one nautical mile per second. Also disclosed was an account of how three experienced air traffic controllers tried to 'talk in' a strange craft that landed on the runway in front of them. This occurred at an airfield in East Anglia in mid-April 1984.[3]

The South Wales Police later issued a curious statement about the June 2008 incident when we contacted its headquarters in Bridgend. Among our enquiries was a clear question as to whether the helicopter's crew, or its base, reported the incident to either the RAF or the MoD.[4] The police, through spokesperson Judith Hammett, supplied a one-page statement concerning the incident, which said that it 'was not a police matter' and that it had not merited any pocket notebook entries. Nor was there any need to 'submit any reports or record anything' on the force's systems.[5]

These comments came in the latter half of the page-long statement, entitled 'Freedom of Information Position'. The earlier 'Public Position' section, however, confirmed that the Air Support Unit did, indeed, sight an 'unusual aircraft' that night. It said the police helicopter did not chase or follow it across the Bristol Channel and over the North Devon coastline, but that the pilot contacted the 'relevant authorities' so that they could investigate further.

The existence of confidentiality clauses prevented any useful comment being made subsequently by Bond Air Services, the company that was operating the helicopter on behalf of the South Wales Police. Neither could it be ascertained from David Wilson, the company's director

Gloucestershire Airport
Staverton
Cheltenham
Gloucestershire
GL51 6SP

Telephone: 01452 856007
Telefax: 01452 856595
www.bondairservices.com

DW/akd/028.09

29 January 2009

Mr D Butler

Dublin
Ireland

Dear Mr Butler

We refer to your letter dated 22 January 2009, which was addressed to our sister company, Bond Offshore Helicopters Limited, but which was passed on to us as we operate the South Wales Police helicopter.

Flight safety is, of course, our primary concern and we can confirm that, where necessary, our pilots file reports on incidents to the CAA in accordance with the applicable regulations. However, the nature of our operations for South Wales Police and the confidentiality provisions of our contract with them mean that we are unable to comment or provide information on specific operations.

With regard to your question in respect of a police helicopter flight over the West Bromwich area, we can advise that we do not operate or provide pilots for the police helicopter covering this area.

Yours sincerely

DAVID WILSON
DIRECTOR OF CONTRACTS
BOND AVIATION GROUP

of contracts, what was described in its pilot's reporting of the incident – nor, indeed, could it be ascertained *which* authorities the pilot contacted.[6]

The May–June 2008 issue of the UK's *UFO DATA* magazine also followed this story and received similar comments from the South Wales Police press office. Oonagh Moore, on behalf of that office, confirmed that the South and East Wales Air Support Unit – the body serves both the South Wales and Gwent police forces – did see an unusual aircraft, but overall her comments mirrored what Judith Hammett had said. *Sun* reporter John Coles, when contacted by *UFO DATA*, insisted that his source was 'well placed' to tell him what had really happened.

SECURITY AND SECRECY

One would think that an unknown aerial craft or device darting about so close to a military base would have been of considerable defence interest, and that the pilot's report would have found its way to the MoD, either directly or through the military, or to the investigative UK Airprox Board (UKAB) or the UK's Civil Aviation Authority (CAA).

Given such official obfuscation, perhaps it should have come as no surprise, then, that it took about a fortnight for the story to appear in the public domain. If it hadn't done so, it might have disappeared into those 150 files that weren't to be fully declassified until 2012, or into other documentation that would remain buried by officialdom. Perhaps it should have come as no surprise, either, that another British police helicopter incident involving an unknown airborne object, in May 2008, took more than six months to appear in the mass media.

At approximately 9.50 p.m. on 2 May, the pilot of an EC-135 helicopter being operated by the West Midlands Police over the West Bromwich area, was forced to swerve out of the path of an unknown aerial craft. The pilot and the two observers on board all reported seeing an 'aircraft' that displayed two continuous blue-green lights.[7] The pilot spotted the object about 328 feet (100 metres) away from his helicopter and he quickly manoeuvred out of its way. All three witnesses maintained that the object then circled their position, flew towards the north, then back again, before finally flying away.

The pilot and crew initially believed that the object might have been 'sinister', or that someone on the ground was fooling around – albeit very dangerously – by flying a remotely controlled, fixed-wing aircraft 'purposefully' around the helicopter.[8] However, a thermal camera failed to pick up any signs of a motor on the unidentified object, while later flights of the same helicopter discounted the possibility of the object's image having been caused by reflected light flashing off the rotor blades, or internal reflections on the canopy. The crew members were unaware of any detection of the intruder by radar at Birmingham Airport, where their air operations unit was based.

This account cannot be put down merely to press exaggeration. Rather, it is taken from the proceedings of the

UKAB's study of the case, in which the crew members gave their statements about the events. The Airprox Board's deliberations concluded with a statement that the incident involved 'an apparent conflict with an unidentified aircraft displaying non-standard lights'.[9]

In reporting on the episode and the UKAB's findings, the British press pointed out that the police officers were flying at an altitude of 1,500 feet (457 metres) when the incident occurred. The crew members, reflecting human fallibility, had concluded that a model aircraft might have been involved. However, Manny Williamson, the development officer for the British Model Flying Association, had spoken to the UKAB during its investigation. He told the media that at that time of night one couldn't see a flying model aircraft very well, let alone fly one. He commented that not only would the lighting conditions need to be good, but that the maximum height for flying would be a couple of hundred feet (around 60 metres) – and certainly nothing like 1,500 feet (457 metres). The UKAB, jointly funded by the CAA and the MoD, agreed. The Airprox Board concluded that, while a clandestine flight by someone operating a microlight or similar aircraft could not be fully ruled out, it seemed very unlikely that they would circle what they could probably see was a police helicopter.

One wonders why a similar investigation was not, officially at least, carried out in the South Wales case. On 10 March 2009, Peter Hunt, the director of UKAB, wrote to say that his organisation had no record of the Welsh incident.

STATES OF DENIAL

Hillingdon House
Uxbridge
Middlesex UB10 0RU
Tel: Uxbridge (01895) 815120
DFTS: (95232) -6120
Fax: (01895) 815124
E mail: peter.hunt@airproxboard.org.uk

UK AIRPROX BOARD

UKAB/   10 March 2009

Mr Dermot Butler

Dublin ▬ Ireland

Dear Mr. Butler

AIRPROX REPORT(S)

Thank you for your letter of 2ⁿᵈ March regarding two incidents, the first occurring on 2ⁿᵈ May 2008 and the second on or about 7ᵗʰ – 8ᵗʰ June 2008.

Full details of the first of the two incidents to which you refer have been published and are available via the UK Airprox Board website, www.airproxboard.org.uk . Midway down the menu at the left side of the 'Home Page' screen, please select 'Publications' which will take you to our Copyright Notice. If you are content with the conditions of the notice then please click 'Agree' which will take you to a page having three options. The middle one of the three is 'Analysis of Airprox in UK Airspace' which on selection brings up a page with 10 choices: please select the top one, 'Analysis of Airprox in UK Airspace – Jan – Jun 2008 Report Number 20'. Within the aforementioned Report, please refer to Airprox 055/08 which gives details of the 2ⁿᵈ May incident.

As regards the second event, in early June, we have no record of this (all Airprox Reports in respect of June 2008 are within 'Report Number 20' should you wish to browse through them). I have checked on your behalf with CAA and a 'quick check' produced nothing of relevance to your enquiry. Should you wish to have CAA run a more detailed check then please contact:

Safety Data Unit
SIDD
2W Aviation House
Gatwick Airport South
Gatwick
West Sussex RH6 0YR

Please do not hesitate to contact me if you feel that I can assist you further.

Yours sincerely

Peter J Hunt
Director
UK Airprox Board

If unidentified aircraft of any sort can penetrate a country's airspace at will, then such unknowns become matters of national security. In cases involving the close proximity of these objects to military, police or civilian aircraft, they seem to become matters of national secrecy. If this isn't so, then there's a mystery surrounding what became of the reports made to the 'relevant authorities' by the pilot in the South Wales incident, and the distinct lack of public announcements concerning any following investigation. These were two very similar cases, both involving near misses between unidentified aerial craft and police aircraft, with both being duly reported. However, only one of the events – the one that did not involve a defence establishment – remained in the public domain.

At least the British public was told something of these unusual events. On the other side of the Irish Sea, the details of an incident involving an Irish police helicopter and a UAP were buried.

IRISH POLICE HELICOPTER ENCOUNTER

For several years, we were (and still are) in regular communication with a trusted contact within the Irish aviation community. On occasion this contact has given us details of UAP-related incidents that have happened within Irish airspace, or that have involved Irish aircrew elsewhere in the world. And strange events involving law enforcement helicopters, like those in England and Wales, are not unknown on the other side of the Irish Sea. Our contact informed us of an unexplained aerial object that had been approached by an EC-135 helicopter being operated by the Air Support Unit of the Garda Síochána (Irish police) over Dublin.[10]

This claim needed to be put on the record while it was still fresh in the mind of our contact. Within days we had the full details of his report of an event that had allegedly occurred over the Howth peninsula area of north Dublin:

> On the evening of 21 August 2006, at around 20.10 or 20.15, I recorded a transmission being sent to aircraft 255, which I believe is the Garda helicopter. It was asked to look at an aircraft which was present in the sky in the same spot for five minutes. 255 was also aware of the aircraft in the same part of the sky. They took up a heading for the aircraft and reported back to the Dublin Airport air traffic control tower that the craft was descending lower on the horizon, as if landing. Also, the craft was further away than they first thought. 255 had the craft in sight all the time, but his last transmission back to the tower was that 'that "guy" must have landed. We have lost sight of him.' The helicopter then got a call to go to an incident in Blanchardstown [in west Dublin], and that ended the transmission.[11]

Our contact's claim was fascinating, but some sort of support, if not verification, was needed. Given the accuracy of data supplied by our contact before and since this incident, and the fact that the Howth area had seen repeated UAP activity in the past, this event merited further enquiries. Here was an incident which, if true, occurred in controlled airspace on the approach to Dublin Airport. The presence of an unknown, hovering craft in this area would be of some concern to air traffic controllers – which it was, as they tasked a law enforcement aircraft with investigating it. However, the safety of other aircraft coming into the area would not have been the sole consideration. There would have been, indeed *should* have been, others. What if the unidentified craft was being flown as part of a terrorist plot? Previously, when Ireland had the temporary presidency of the European Union, the Irish Aviation Authority (IAA) had established a Temporary Restricted Area (TRA) around the Irish capital. Flights within the TRA had to be authorised specifically by a senior official in the Security and Northern Ireland Division of the country's Department of Justice, Equality and Law Reform. The TRA was put in place by the IAA with the consent of the then Minister for Transport, Seamus Brennan. The only exemptions to this security measure were state aircraft and flights by the Irish Coast Guard.[12] While this restriction was lifted at the end of the country's EU presidency, it demonstrates how seriously the nation was taking the threat of terrorism from the air. In the post-9/11 era, such an attitude had not changed and at the time of writing it still hasn't.

If the unidentified craft had no flight plan and no transponder, the possibility would also have arisen that it was possibly smuggling. People, weapons, illegal cash or drugs might have been coming into the country, yet none of this is mentioned in the reported radio exchange between the control tower and the helicopter. It should be noted, too, that the object was further away than was first thought, and that it was seen to descend, as if landing. Yet the only thing to land on, beyond Howth, is the Irish Sea. How could it have landed there? If the unknown craft was an aircraft in distress and it had crashed into the sea beyond Howth, then either the control tower or the helicopter would have taken action by contacting the rescue services. The report and the subsequent written statement by our contact didn't mention anything in this regard. Nor did any media reports in the following days mention any searches or rescue activity off the Dublin coast.

The Garda Air Support Unit's (GASU) assets – including the aircraft involved, which has since been replaced – are flown by military pilots stationed at the Irish Air Corps base at Baldonnel, south Dublin. It was to the GASU at this base that we sent a written request for information, but we received no response.[13] It seemed unusual, whether the incident had occurred or not, that no one would issue even a brief statement on behalf of the GASU. Even if our contact's claim was incorrect, a brief comment from the unit could have put the matter to rest. Its lack of response necessitated, instead, repeated queries to be forwarded to both garda headquarters and the Air Corps.[14]

The approach to garda headquarters prompted a reply, with our queries having then been passed back to the GASU at Baldonnel, which then issued a one-page statement. Sergeant Donal Doyle wrote that he could find 'no reference' to a garda aircraft answering a request from Dublin air traffic control (ATC) to help identify an aircraft on or about 21 August. The GASU, he went on, had on occasion been asked to identify aircraft that had strayed into the Dublin

Garda Air Support Unit
Casement Aerodrome,
Baldonnel
Dublin 22.

Mr. Dermot Butler

Dublin

Re: Incident on or about the 21ˢᵗ August 2006.

Dear Sir,

I wish to acknowledge receipt of your letter dated the 29ᵗʰ April 2007 and to state that having checked the records at the Garda Air Support Unit I could find no reference to attending to a request from Dublin ATC to assist in identifying an aircraft over Howth Head on or about the 21ˢᵗ August 2006.

The Garda Air Support Unit has in the past been requested by Dublin ATC to assist with identifying aircraft which encroach on the Dublin Terminal Control Area without prior radio contact. In these cases it has been found that the encroaching aircraft were hot air balloons which because of adverse wind conditions have strayed into controlled air space.

I hope that this information will be of assistance to you and if I can be of any further help I can be contacted at the above address.

Yours.

Sergeant
(Donal Doyle)

terminal control area without contacting the ATC tower by radio beforehand. On these occasions, the aircraft turned out to be hot air balloons that had been blown into controlled airspace by adverse wind conditions.[15]

Initially, this seemed reasonable. However, a hot air balloon would not normally have been flying in that area and at such an hour. More importantly, Doyle passed no comment on one key query: the unidentified airborne object's loss of altitude, with nothing but the Irish Sea below it.

Three weeks after contacting the Air Corps, its press officer responded that he had found 'no record' of the Air Corps having been notified about the sighting. Commandant E. Murphy also stated that on the pertinent date and on the previous and subsequent days, there were no records of any reports from the watch manager at Dublin Airport about the sighting. (Interestingly, Murphy mentioned in his reply that our query had related to 'an aircraft picked up on radar' that night. We had never stated that it had definitely been detected in this way, as neither we nor our contact knew for sure.) Commandant Murphy went to the effort of speaking to the GASU crew who had been on duty on the night in question. None of its members could recall the incident, with the pilot remembering, instead, another event that had occurred around the same date. However, this incident had involved a hot air balloon to the west of Dublin Airport, flying outside the Dublin control zone.[16]

Having contacted the Air Corps and the Garda Air Support Unit, the only conclusion to be reached was that

Ceanncheathrú an Aerchóir
Aeradróm Mhic Easmuinn
Baile Dhónaill
Baile Átha Cliath 22
Éire.

Air Corps Headquarters
Casement Aerodrome
Baldonnel
Dublin 22
Ireland.

Tel: + 353 1 403 7512
Fax: + 353 1 403 7850
Email: eamonn.murphy@defenceforces.ie

21st May 2007

Dermot Butler.

Dublin

RE: UNIDENTIFIED AIRCRAFT

1. I refer to your recent query concerning an aircraft picked up on radar by Air Traffic Control at Dublin on the evening of 21st August 2006.

2. Again, as with your previous query, I have checked through our records for the day concerned (and additionally the previous and following day) and we have no record of being notified or receiving any reports from the Watch Manager at Dublin airport concerning this sighting.

3. The aircraft concerned (if operating in the Howth area) would have been operating in the Dublin Air Traffic Control Zone so I would assume that the Watch Manager on the evening concerned would have followed this incident up with the Irish Aviation Authority.

4. I have spoken to the aircrew of the Garda Air Support Unit who were on duty on the evening concerned and they cannot recall specifically this incident. The pilot concerned however does recall around the same date being asked by Dublin Air Traffic Control to see if they could identify an object which had appeared on their radar screens but it was West of the airport as opposed to East. On the evening in question the aircrew on duty identified this radar return as a hot air balloon operating west of the airport just outside the Dublin Control Zone.

5. Once again, unfortunately we have not been able to assist you in conclusively providing an answer to your query but maybe Dublin Air Traffic Control or the Irish Aviation Authority may be in a position to shed some further light on this, if indeed it was further investigated.

E. Murphy
Comdt.
Press Officer
Irish Air Corps

Irish Coast Guard
GARDA CÓSTA na hÉIREANN

Dermot Butler

████████████

Dublin ██   18/07/2007

Dear Dermot,

Sorry for the delay in replying to your letter. I thought it had already been replied to. I am afraid I do not have a lot of information for you.

Ref the article in the Sunday Independent on the 4th Feb:
MRCC did get 'flare' reports on the 1st and 2nd Feb. These were in the Wicklow and Wexford area. These areas were searched but there was nothing unusual found.
On the 3rd the stations at Valentia and Malinhead got several reports of flares from Ballycotton in Cork around the south and west coast up to Bundoran in Donegal. This was put down to meteorite activity.

Ref the unidentified aircraft off Howth.
I'm afraid we have no information on this. The Coast Guard or RNLI were not informed of this. Maybe ATC in Dublin could help you.
You are correct in saying that the Garda Helicopter is not equipped to fly over large expanses of water.

If you require any more information you can contact me on the address below.

Yours Sincerely,

Ger Hegarty
Divisional Controller
MRCC Dublin
Irish Coast Guard
Leeson Lane
Dublin 2

the incident simply didn't happen. If an aircraft of any sort was seen by a garda aircraft to descend over the open water of the Irish Sea, or if even a flare was spotted by its crew, then the very least that should have happened would have been that either the Irish Coast Guard or the Royal National Lifeboat Institute (RNLI) – or both – would have been alerted. This did not happen, according to Ger Hegarty, the divisional controller of the Coast Guard's Marine Rescue Co-ordination Centre (MRCC) in Dublin. The files of the MRCC held no references either to the Coast Guard or the RNLI having been informed about any such sighting.[17]

The only question remaining concerns a fact we hadn't included in the queries that were presented to those who piloted and crewed the garda aircraft, because there should not have been any need to mention it … if the incident did not occur, if the Dublin Airport control tower and the helicopter did not discuss an unknown 'aircraft' over the Howth area, then how was it that the conversation was *recorded*?

The recording made for very interesting listening and it confirmed the authenticity of our contact's original claim that the episode had, in fact, taken place. A transcript of the relevant portion of the supplied recording is reproduced below:

TOWER: If you could go up there at high speed, I have traffic just swinging around Howth.

255: Roger. We'll give you our best speed anyway. 255.

TOWER: Clear, 255. Do you see that below …?

255: Affirm. See him descending now. He is just gone below the horizon.

TOWER: Okay … eh, 255, thank you.

255: Roger. We will keep heading down that direction anyway.

TOWER: 255, is that in your eh … eh … on the nose of your aircraft now?

255: Yeah … he's in about our half twelve/one o'clock now …

255: Tower, 255. He seems to be getting lower all the time there. He's probably landing.

TOWER: Roger. Thank you.

TOWER: 255, have you reached that site yet?

255: We'll be there in about two minutes.

A silence then follows between the control tower and the helicopter, which lasts over a minute and a half, then:

TOWER: Oh! It's further out than I thought.

255: It is, yeah …

255: Tower, 255.

TOWER: 255.

255: That guy appears to have landed. We have lost sight of him now at this stage, and, eh, we have another call in the Blanchardstown area. Not above a thousand [1,000 feet].

TOWER: Roger, 255. Cleared to Blanchardstown.

255: Roger, cleared to Blanchardstown, 255.

The identity of the intruder and where it landed – if, indeed, it did land – remain unanswered questions. Why there was no follow-up by the authorities is also a mystery. The use of the word 'guy' is unusual in aviation parlance, and its use to represent an unknown aerial object prompts the idea that all of those involved may well have known what the object *wasn't*, that it was not merely a conventional aircraft, but that they would not openly say so over the airwaves. After all, if there was even the remotest possibility that what was seen was an aircraft in distress, or a flare from a boat in need of assistance, then the sea rescue authorities would surely have been contacted immediately. According to the Air Corps, the watch manager at Dublin Airport did not file a report in relation to the incident, while the aircrew could apparently recall other incidents, but not this one. Officialdom decreed that it did not happen, yet the whole episode was recorded.

2

BEAMS

The existence of an unidentified airborne object in Irish airspace – which seemed to drift further away when approached by a police helicopter – serves as a reminder that unexplained phenomena *do* occur in the skies of the world's nations. Ireland is not alone in having to deal with this fact, as the two events concerning the British police have shown. Only one of these, involving the West Midlands Police, appeared in the records of the UKAB (report file No. 055/08), while the incident involving a police aircraft near an RAF facility in South Wales seems to have been airbrushed from public awareness.

It would seem that, in the corridors of power, information about certain aspects of the UAP topic is not being passed on to the general public. Investigations can either be shifted 'upstairs' or they are stopped in their tracks completely, because it is probably realised that there is little or nothing that can be done about what is being observed.

Gary Heseltine, a serving member of the UK's Transport

Police and founder of the Police Reporting UFOs (PRUFOS) website, has reported on one such case. At 2.25 a.m. on 17 November 2003, two adults and a child watched between twenty and thirty red-and-white flashing objects in the sky over the Bromley area of Kent, in southern England. They heard a whirring noise coming from the objects and captured them on videotape. The trio reported their sighting to the police and an officer was dispatched to look into it. The officer, who was a sergeant at Scotland Yard, also saw the flashing objects. Using a lamp post as a reference point, the sergeant could see that the movements of these objects included zigzag manoeuvres and turns across the sky, which were estimated to be faster than the movements of any conventional aircraft.

The Kent police helicopter was notified and its crew confirmed that its members could see the objects, but they assumed that they might have been aircraft inbound to Heathrow Airport. The police subsequently contacted the Swanwick Military ATC centre, which stated that the only aircraft in the area were at a high altitude and not at the lower altitudes that were indicated by the civilian and police witnesses on the ground. Also, there were no radar returns detected where the flashing objects were being observed. By 4 a.m. Swanwick had been in touch with RAF Neatishead about the objects, and at 6.12 a.m. a report on the incident was submitted to the MoD's Directorate of Air Staff by the RAF base.

Under the UK's freedom of information legislation,

Gary Heseltine was successful in obtaining several documents pertaining to the incident. The odd sighting did not, he discovered, have any meaningful follow-up official investigation. The radar tapes for the area, for the particular time of the sighting, were reviewed. With only routine air traffic having been recorded, nothing 'of defence interest' had been detected and there, apparently, the matter was dropped.

Heseltine, a former serving member of the RAF, found this attitude 'staggering'. Understandably so, given the view of officialdom that if formations of twenty or thirty aerial craft or devices of some sort don't show up on radar, then they couldn't *possibly* pose a threat! This verdict of senior military officers or defence officials, not to pursue the civilians' video images of the formation – let alone ascertain if any relevant footage was shot by the police helicopter crew – ought to concern us all.[1]

It seems strange that a large group of unidentified objects over Kent, which could zigzag at velocities that were described as faster than any conventional aircraft, was never investigated by the British defence establishment. It is as though the authorities already knew what these objects were *not* – that is, conventional (earthly) technology. Again, investigations either reach a cut-off point, beyond which the press and public alike are given no answers as the research continues further on up the ladder of intelligence or military hierarchies, or else those same authorities genuinely stop probing cases where the answer is obvious to them.

There is a suspicion that this may have been the case

with the Irish police helicopter incident at Howth, Dublin. If so, then the approach of Ireland's authorities is the same as almost anywhere else in the world.

This becomes a problem, though, when unknown flying objects become more difficult to explain. Stars, meteors, aircraft filmed at odd angles, aircraft lights and birds have invariably been thrown into the mix to try to explain away the thornier cases – or to ridicule witnesses. The popular craze in recent years for releasing Chinese (sky) lanterns at social occasions has also been suggested as a one-size-fits-all 'solution' to the puzzle. The problem arises when these things form a triangular shape in the sky ... and then proceed to project beams of light.

On 3 August 2008, a Sunday, a member of the Irish police had an experience that will live long in his memory. At a little after 10.30 p.m., he was driving south through the County Meath town of Dunboyne when he noticed several groups of white objects in the sky in front of him. They were in formations of three, moving from his right to left, and as the fourth group came into view over a wooded area on the far side of a junction, he had an opportunity to pull in to the side of the road. Climbing out of his vehicle, he activated the camera on his mobile phone and managed to capture a fascinating sequence.

With the ticking of his car's indicators audible in the background, the footage showed three bright white objects, in a triangular formation, gliding to the left and rotating slightly in unison as they did so. Before the sequence ended, the object furthest to the left of the screen emitted a thin, sharply defined, bright red beam of light, which darted towards the ground. It lasted just a fraction of a second. As far as the police officer could discern, the formation made no noise.

LOCAL NETWORKS

Since we established UFO and Paranormal Research Ireland (UPRI) in November 1998, a network of local researchers has been established around both the Republic of Ireland and Northern Ireland, whose task it is to conduct enquiries and witness interviews in local areas on our behalf. It was through this arrangement that we secured the footage directly from the officer in Dunboyne within twenty-four hours of the event. The garda was ridiculed by some of his friends and colleagues when he told them about what he had seen and recorded. We therefore agreed to his request for anonymity from the very start.

At the 2008 annual Irish UFO conference, hosted by the late Betty Meyler, of the UFO Society of Ireland, we were first able to present the images to the public. Carl Nally's presentation generated considerable interest from both the attending public and the media, with Dermot Butler joining in in responding to a large number of questions from the attendees.

The press presence had been triggered, in no small way, by a piece that the *Irish Daily Star* journalist Kevin Jenkinson had penned the previous Friday, in which he correctly pointed out that the three bright objects actually looked to be illuminated corner points of a single, large, triangular object in the night sky.[2] On 27 September, *The Irish Sun* ran a full-page item headed 'Take Meath to Your Leader', written by Myles McEntee. It gave a quite balanced view of what the video's images depicted and reproduced a frame we had supplied from the footage, which showed the exact moment that the red beam appeared.[3]

These two news items reached the newsstands *before* the footage had actually been shown. The press reaction afterwards was more important, if the public was to be given an unbiased view of what had been recorded on that Sunday night almost two months earlier. Broadly speaking, the media reaction was positive in the days that followed. On 29 September Kevin Jenkinson wrote a short piece about the recording having been shown and about the conference overall. In the *Irish Independent* on the same date, meanwhile, reporter Anita Guidera outlined, again, what the footage showed. Her comments were to the point, factual and accurate.[4] Almost a week later the *Sunday World* tabloid was less so, but its reporter at the conference, Geraldine Comiskey, at least went to the effort of making herself known, approaching the speakers and attendees alike and introducing herself. In fairness, her report reflected a lack of knowledge about the subject overall, but it was a pleasant surprise to read that her comments on the footage did not immediately follow the tired old route of stating a *definite* link between *unidentified* objects or phenomena in the sky and extraterrestrial spaceships.[5]

On 5 October 2008, the *Sunday Tribune*'s Ken Sweeney published an item about the footage, with a large portion of an inside page optimistically declaring that 'an Irish UFO tape' was to be 'beamed around the world'. The article stated, correctly, that the images would be shown again at a paranormal conference being held the following Saturday, 11 October, at Clontarf Castle in the north of Dublin city. The piece outlined the story behind the footage and quoted one of the organisers of the upcoming conference, Mark Guerin, who said that the event was an opportunity for witnesses to all manner of paranormal phenomena to speak about what they'd experienced.

Unfortunately, the same still images that had been supplied to *The Irish Sun* and the *Irish Daily Star*, and subsequently reproduced there in high-quality detail, didn't fare as well in this newspaper. Rather than showing three sharply defined light sources, this version was extremely blurred, showing three fuzzy and diffuse objects instead. Their clarity had suffered because of a shortcoming in the newspaper's photo reproduction software, as confirmed to us by Sweeney. A green-hued double image rendered the pictures quite useless – especially the frame that had shown the previously clear red beam, but which now consisted of a multicoloured mess.[6]

The following day, we received a phone call (and later an e-mail) from Ken Sweeney, about one particular reaction that had come in to his newspaper's office with regard to his article. The office had been contacted by Andrea Mulligan, a solicitor living in Manchester, UK, who stated that the objects that had been seen were nothing more than part of a group of sky lanterns that had been released at her wedding reception that night. At 10.30 p.m. or so, the band playing at the celebration stopped for a break, so she joined her new husband, Lynden James, and accompanied some guests into the grounds of the Dunboyne Castle Hotel, where they lit and released a number of the devices. This, Mulligan had reasoned with the newspaper, *must* have been what the policeman had recorded.

Ken Sweeney's e-mail was accompanied by three attachments. All three consisted of photographs taken at the wedding reception, with the first of these depicting the smiling bride in the company of others who were, in turn, unfolding a lantern for launch. The other images showed some lanterns, glowing an orange-red colour, gaining altitude a short distance away.

The day after Ken Sweeney got in touch, on 7 October, we were on the telephone to each other, talking about these new developments. While this conversation was continuing on a landline, Carl's mobile phone rang on the table beside him, interrupting our discussion. The caller was Andrea Mulligan, who didn't realise that Dermot could now hear her conversation. Her call was polite, though brief and very much to the point. She repeated what Ken Sweeney had reported – that any mysterious objects over Dunboyne on the night of the previous 3 August were sky lanterns and that was all there was to it.

Carl listened to her, taking on board all of the points she made. It should not have been too difficult therefore to discern how many sky lanterns the wedding party had released. He asked precisely that question, and then attempted to explain that the witness had observed four *groups* of three light sources in each group, crossing the sky in front of him. This gave a total of twelve. However, she interrupted him as soon as he said the word 'four' to her.

There is quite a difference between four objects, and four groups with three objects in *each group*. Andrea Mulligan had emphasised that the former – four – was the correct number of lanterns released. He repeated 'four' to her as a question, and she agreed. So if the wedding party had only released four, then what were the other eight objects? Ms Mulligan had nothing further to add, nor would she comment on the red beam. The conversation ended.

The footage was given its second public showing at the paranormal conference in Dublin. The event, Paracon '08, was put together by Mark Guerin and his colleagues in the humorously named but seriously-intentioned group, PIGs (Paranormal Investigation Guys). Once again, the sequence was explained, shown, and questions and comments were invited afterwards. The day-long event provided ample opportunities to speak with various investigative groups and individual researchers involved in all manner of paranormal investigations. Conspicuous by their absence, however, were members of the media with any interest in the Dunboyne footage. Just one reporter, Warren Swords, had telephoned

Carl shortly before the images were shown. He was working on a piece for the next day's edition of the *Irish Mail
on Sunday*, and had been on the telephone, off and on, for
the previous three or four days. The reason for the dearth of
press interest would become clear the following morning.

The headline 'Bride Shoots Down UFOs' on the next
day's *Sunday Times* summed up the new, overall attitude of
the print media. With almost half of an inside page dedicated to continuing the headline story, the newspaper's
Colin Coyle opted for Andrea Mulligan's version of events.
He rightly pointed out that a video of the Dunboyne sighting had been shown at Paracon '08 the day before and the
bride was quoted as saying that 'about twenty-five' lanterns
were released at the wedding reception. Furthermore, the
journalist quoted her as saying that 'we've seen the images
and there's no doubt about it: they're our lanterns'. While
the wedding party had obtained permission from the Irish
Aviation Authority to release the sixty lanterns they pos-
sessed, the weather was 'so gusty' they decided to release
'only about twenty-five' of them.[7]

The official permission to release sixty lanterns was
echoed by Warren Swords in his *Irish Mail on Sunday*
feature of the same date. He quoted Andrea Mulligan as
having said that 'only twenty' were actually launched. She
was also quoted as saying that the police witness had filmed
four of them. (How it was that four of them could make
up the recorded triangle, with just the three corners of that
triangle being illuminated, was anyone's guess.) So, the total

of 'about twenty-five' had become 'only twenty' – after the total of 'four' had been confirmed to Carl on the telephone five days previously.[8]

If the amount of lanterns released could vary so wildly – with all the different figures apparently coming from just one person who was present at their launch – it didn't augur too well for the overall accuracy of the resulting press reports … but worse was to come. It will be remembered that, in response to the *Sunday Tribune* article of a week earlier, photographs of several of the lanterns in mid-air were sent to the paper by Andrea Mulligan and these were then sent on to us. The lanterns were reddish in colour, and *not* bright white, as captured in the garda's footage. Colin Coyle had failed to pick up on this point in his *Sunday Times* article, as had Warren Swords in the *Irish Mail on Sunday*. Indeed, Swords' piece was written up and submitted for publication after he had telephoned Carl at the Paracon '08 event, but his newspaper had failed to send Swords along to actually view the footage for himself. Colin Coyle hadn't seen it either – and, crucially, neither had Andrea Mulligan. She had only seen the two blurry stills in the 5 October *Sunday Tribune* item by Ken Sweeney and her resulting opinion was then accepted by the two newspaper features the following Sunday. None of them had seen the actual footage, including the beam being emitted during that footage.

As all of this newspaper coverage was going on, various internet paranormal discussion forums sprang to life, with opinions varying – as always in cyberspace – from the

sublime to the ridiculous. The internet is a valuable communication and research tool, but its downside is that hoaxers
and armchair critics, who are apparently experts on everything and who can never admit to being wrong about anything, populate swathes of it. Attempting to debate the facts
and the images was a waste of time and effort as far as we
were concerned, but in fairness to *The Sunday Times*, its edition of 19 October reproduced a selection of the messages it
had received electronically in the week since Colin Coyle's
article had appeared.

One contributor to the paper's 'Message Board' column,
named simply as 'Amanda', referred to the discrepancy in
the number of lanterns released. The twenty-five (or so) in
the previous Sunday's issue of the paper had now changed,
yet again, to just twelve in an on-line comment Andrea
Mulligan had posted during the week.[9] Mulligan's tally was
previously 'about' twenty-five, or twenty, or four. After Carl
had spoken with her on the telephone, trying to tell her of
the four groups with three objects in each group – giving
a total of twelve – her latest version now reflected that
number.

This story is also important for another reason: the lack
of wisdom on the part of the IAA in allowing the release of
sky lanterns – up to sixty of them were authorised – just 8
miles or so (some 13 kilometres) from Dublin Airport. The
Dunboyne area, indeed, is on a flight path which constitutes
an approach to, or a climb-out from, Ireland's largest and
busiest airport. It seemed incredible that the authorities

MET ÉIREANN
The Irish Meteorological Service

Glasnevin Hill,	Cnoc Ghlas Naíon,	Tel: +353-1-806 4200
Dublin 9, Ireland.	Baile Átha Cliath 9, Éire.	Fax: +353-1-806 4247

Our Reference: WS1730/0901

8th January 2009

Mr Graham Meates

Dublin ▓

Dear Mr Meates
With reference to your letter of 2nd January, I enclose hourly wind direction data for Dublin Airport for the evening hours of the week-end of 2nd/3rd August 2008.

Yours faithfully

Niall Brooks
Niall Brooks
Climatological Division

```
+---------------------------+-------------+-----------------------------------+
|date                       |direction    |name                               |
+---------------------------+-------------+-----------------------------------+
|02-aug-2008 18:00:00       |         240 |Dublin Airport                     |
|02-aug-2008 19:00:00       |         260 |Dublin Airport                     |
|02-aug-2008 20:00:00       |         240 |Dublin Airport                     |
|02-aug-2008 21:00:00       |         250 |Dublin Airport                     |
|02-aug-2008 22:00:00       |         250 |Dublin Airport                     |
|02-aug-2008 23:00:00       |         240 |Dublin Airport                     |
|03-aug-2008 18:00:00       |         250 |Dublin Airport                     |
|03-aug-2008 19:00:00       |         260 |Dublin Airport                     |
|03-aug-2008 20:00:00       |         260 |Dublin Airport                     |
|03-aug-2008 21:00:00       |         250 |Dublin Airport                     |
|03-aug-2008 22:00:00       |         240 |Dublin Airport                     |
|03-aug-2008 23:00:00       |         240 |Dublin Airport                     |
+---------------------------+-------------+-----------------------------------+
```

could allow up to sixty lanterns to be released so close to various flight paths around the capital's airport. Such devices, even if they didn't reach the airport itself, would have appeared precisely where aircraft would have been either gaining altitude or preparing to land. In essence, the flight path would have been a minefield, with every passing aircraft being in danger.

This was an extremely serious matter. After all, sky lanterns can possibly reach 2,000–3,000 feet (610–914 metres) in altitude – Colin Coyle went for the latter figure in his 12 October *Sunday Times* piece – and the thought of them being sucked into an aircraft's engine is a terrifying one. Media reports had pointed out that Andrea Mulligan and Lynden James had obtained permission from the IAA and from the Garda Síochána to release their lanterns. In early 2009 we sought a response from the police station in Dunboyne about this.[10]

In January and April 2009, Niall Brooks of the Climatological Division of Met Éireann, Ireland's national weather service, told us that the wind direction recorded at Dublin Airport between 6 p.m. and 11 p.m. on the previous 3 August had been 240 to 260 degrees. The breeze was coming across the country from the North Atlantic, through the Dunboyne area. The wind speed, incidentally, was ten knots between 10.30 p.m. and 10.50 p.m. that night.[11]

If it was gusty, one would think that the microphone on the policeman's phone would have recorded this. It didn't, even though the ticking of his car's indicators were heard clearly. Also, one would think that the three bright light sources he recorded – which, again, were white, and not orange or red – would have drifted about aimlessly. They didn't, and they turned slowly in unison, as if what was being observed was indeed one large, triangular object.

Meanwhile, Graham Meates, a north Dublin resident, had been watching with interest as the story unfolded in the press. The idea of launching lanterns at a wedding or other social gathering appealed to him, so in November 2008, and again in January 2009, he wrote to the IAA to ask how he should go about obtaining official permission to do so. He received no replies.[12]

At the end of March 2009, however, we took a telephone call from the Dunboyne garda station. Speaking on behalf of a superintendent, the caller stated that we had received no reply to our repeated queries because such launches were not within the force's jurisdiction.[13] If it was outside the area of responsibility of the Garda Síochána, then there was no need for members of the wedding party to seek police permission, as they had done according to press reports. Another complication came from the IAA in May 2009, when Tony Harkin of its Flight Operations Department contacted Dermot Butler to say that permission had been sought in writing, on 18 March the previous year. Permission was given on 2 April … for *fifty* lanterns![14]

Once again, the number of lanterns had changed. To put an end to this question, and to establish why a potential death trap was allowed to float up through a flight path,

BEAMS

IRISH AVIATION AUTHORITY
ÚDARÁS EITLÍOCHTA NA hÉIREANN

AVIATION HOUSE, HAWKINS STREET, DUBLIN 2, IRELAND
TEL: (01) 671 8655   FAX: (01) 679 2934

Mr. Dermot Butler,

Dublin ▓

Flight Operations Department.

13th May, 2009.

Re: Sky Lanterns

Dear Mr. Butler,

I refer to your letter dated 8th April, 2009 to the Authority regarding the launching of "Chinese Sky Lanterns" which were released from Dunboyne Castle on Sunday 3rd August, 2008.

The request to launch 50 lanterns was made in writing to the Authority on 18th March, 2008. Consultation with all relevant parties took place on the matter upon receipt of the specific request and permission for the launch was given by the Authority on 2nd April, 2008 for the launch to take place in August 3rd at Dunboyne Castle.

Yours sincerely,

Tony Harkin
FOD IAA

it was necessary to contact both Andrea Mulligan and the Irish government's then transport minister, Noel Dempsey.

In April 2010, John Scarry, a researcher based in north County Wicklow, with whom we had liaised about various incidents since the early 1990s, contacted us. He too had been watching closely as the Dunboyne episode was repeatedly mentioned in the press or dusted off and commented about online. He decided to trace Andrea Mulligan and wrote to her at her Manchester office. Within days she replied and he passed her handwritten response on to us. Her letter, dated 16 April, mentioned dealing with Tony Harkin of the IAA. And she gave the figure for the lanterns as fifty. Yet the newspapers that had tried to ridicule the police officer's sighting and had spoken with Ms Mulligan, had insisted the number was sixty. So, apparently, there *weren't* sixty lanterns after all, the police *weren't* involved in granting any permission, the recorded airborne objects were white and not even remotely red or orange ... and *none* of those propagating the sceptical view of the footage had ever seen the sequence before passing judgement on it.

Stanton Friedman, a veteran Canadian researcher, has said in interviews and presentations that when the media – and therefore much of the public – go for the easy option of not actually examining what was seen (or recorded) before dismissing an entire event out of hand, they are in effect saying 'don't bother me with the facts, my mind is made up'. This attitude had gained traction internationally, once clumsily faked renditions of the Dunboyne footage appeared on the internet. Even seasoned investigators such as Russel Callaghan, formerly of Britain's popular *UFO Magazine*, took the bait on this occasion. Indeed, some decidedly dodgy footage was shown at an annual UFO conference in Laughlin, Nevada, USA, in early 2009. The presenter's mistaken belief, that *this* was the Dunboyne footage and that it had fooled UPRI, came about because he had believed nonsense that had been placed on the internet.

Here hoaxers were muddying the waters, and it happened in spite of the efforts of an English UFO researcher, Valerie Young, to clarify things with a widely circulated e-mail to other investigators. Unlike all of the vociferous doubters who blindly toed the 'sky lantern' line, she had travelled to the Irish UFO conference to view the recording for herself.[15]

In June 2009 the Irish government's transport minister, Noel Dempsey, wrote us a two-page letter explaining how sky lanterns are constructed and how they operate. This data was not requested. He also included some details of the application process that had been employed for permission to launch such devices by Andrea Mulligan's wedding party. This data *had been* requested. He outlined (as did the IAA's Tony Harkin) how a request to launch fifty of them was received by the IAA in March of the previous year. Dempsey's letter also pointed out that those wishing to launch the lanterns were requested to get in touch with Dublin ATC one hour beforehand, to ensure that safety would not be compromised. The minister also stated that

Office of the Minister
Transport House, Kildare Street, Dublin 2, Ireland.

Oifig an Aire
Teach Iompair, Sráid Chill Dara, Baile Átha Cliath 2, Éire.

Department of Transport
An Roinn Iompair

Tel: +353 1 670 7444   Locall: 1890 443311   Fax: +353 1 604 1183   Web: www.transport.ie   Email: minister@transport.ie

17 June 2009

Mr. Dermot Butler

Dublin

Dear Mr. Butler,

I refer further to your letter dated 15 May 2009 and regret the delay in responding.

I can confirm that officials from my Department sent a letter to the Irish Aviation Authority (IAA) following receipt of your initial correspondence requesting information in relation to the matter in question. My officials have now been provided with information about "sky lanterns" and answers to the questions you raised in your subsequent letter dated 15 May 2009 which I will outline below.

I understand from the IAA that that launch of these lanterns pose no threat to aircraft or passengers on aircraft, they are launch all over the world and our neighbouring Authority, the UK CAA, issue permissions for their launch on a very regular basis.

I have been advised by the IAA that sky lanterns are constructed of rice paper and brittle wood (frame) into which is placed a small candle. When released the lighted candle heats the air contained in the lantern and it gently rises/floats into the night air. When the candle is exhausted the lantern falls safely to the ground and because it is biodegradable it rots. If the wind is too strong when the lanterns are released the candle will not remain lighted.

A request for permission to launch fifty of these lanterns was made to the IAA, in writing, on 18th March 2008. On receipt of this request Mr. Harkin consulted with a number of colleagues within the Authority to ascertain if these lanterns are considered significant obstacles or any form of threat to air safety, the response he received from his colleagues was that air safety would not be compromised.

A letter granting permission to launch fifty lanterns issued on 2nd April 2008, the permission requested the applicant to contact Dublin Air Traffic Control one hour prior to launch and stated that ATC instructions must be followed as final decision on the launch of the lanterns rested with ATC. I am assured that should meteorological factors on a particular day militate against a particular launch the ATC will not give final approval.

The IAA has advised me that the Gardaí have no role in relation to the grant of permission to launch lanterns. Furthermore they have also informed me that the UK Civil Aviation Authority Safety Regulation Group and Rolls Royce Engineering have determined that ingestion of balloons or sky lanterns would not have detrimental effect on a turbine engine's performance regardless of its passage through the engine.

In light of the information that the IAA has provided I am satisfied that their decision to grant such a permission was made entirely on the basis that air safety would not be compromised in any way.

I trust that this has addressed your concerns.

Yours sincerely,

Noel Dempsey, T.D.
Minister for Transport

the IAA advised him that the Garda Síochána 'have no role in relation to the grant [*sic*] of permission to launch lanterns'.

The minister was 'satisfied' with the IAA's decision to grant permission for the launch of this large number of lanterns. However, neither he nor the IAA, which was contacted by his officials before he drafted his reply, answered any queries concerning the wind speed and direction on the relevant night. Nor did they address the fact that one manufacturer's website had stated that its lanterns had a ceiling of 1,500 metres (around 4,900 feet) and could burn for up to twenty minutes. How could this *not* be a threat to aircraft?[16]

Finally, Dempsey commented on the materials used in the manufacture of sky lanterns, with rice paper, a candle and brittle wood being mentioned. The IAA informed him that the UK CAA's Safety Regulation Group and Rolls-Royce Engineering had both determined that the intake of balloons or sky lanterns would not have an adverse effect on a turbine engine's performance. We attempted to get Rolls-Royce and the CAA to elaborate on this assertion, but neither responded.[17]

One crucial component was missing from the minister's parts list for sky lanterns: metal wire. Also missing from his reply was any reference to what could happen to *various* aircraft, with different engine types. No one knew what types of aircraft might be traversing the Dunboyne area that night. Anything from jet airliners to small planes or helicopters could have been there when a group of sky lanterns came up to their altitude to meet them.

Overall, what occurred was a quite alarming sequence of events, where an aviation disaster of unprecedented seriousness might well have happened west of Dublin Airport. Events outside Ireland in 2009 and beyond serve as a warning about this. For example, in July 2009, a wedding in Italy ended in mayhem when the bride and groom hired a small plane, from which the bride wished to throw her bouquet to a line of women guests below. Passenger Isidoro Pensieri was badly injured when the flowers were sucked into the engine, which exploded. The aircraft caught fire and crashed. It was believed that the flowers were bound with metal ties.[18]

In the opening weeks of 2011, the CAA published new safety regulations that were designed to eliminate risks posed to aircraft by sky lanterns – lanterns which, we had been told, posed no threat in Irish airspace. The CAA warned that the devices could pose a risk if they were sucked into the engines of commercial aircraft.[19] In February 2011, Manchester Airport's operations director, Tim McDermott, highlighted that even small metal fragments posed a threat to aircraft safety and that pilots had encountered lanterns at several thousand feet (hundreds of metres) up. The dangers had already seen some European countries, including Germany and Austria, banning the launching of lanterns.[20]

Three months before Noel Dempsey's response, *Daily Telegraph* correspondent Malcolm Moore had reported that there was a blanket ban imposed on launching lanterns in the Sanya Island area of China, after no fewer than sixty-one flights had been delayed that year because of the presence of lanterns close to flight paths.[21]

Readers can form their own opinions regarding the shortcomings in Ireland's aviation regulations and safety procedures from all of this, while the actual Dunboyne footage may be studied on the internet. It has been uploaded on to the YouTube website. (It was also placed on the UPRI website – see our contact details at the end of the book.) The garda witnessing the Dunboyne incident proves that ordinary people can and do experience extraordinary phenomena in the sky. A cursory search through our files yielded many cases that readily demonstrated this fact. A few examples are related below.

AERIAL INTRUSIONS

A young Polish woman walking through Dublin's city centre in July 2007 was stunned to see a large, black, triangular object hovering overhead. Karolina Dudek later commented that what she observed over the city on a bright summer's afternoon had 'really frightened' her, as the triangle – from which she could discern no noise above the sounds of traffic – had accelerated from a standstill to disappearing from sight in a matter of about three seconds as it darted towards the Irish Sea.[22]

A similar ability to accelerate away at incredible speed was evident in August 2008, when Keith Mooney was driving his mother home from a social engagement she had attended in Dublin's north-western suburb of Finglas. His sighting also occurred in daylight as he drove east across the northern city suburbs, from Finglas through Ballymun, then on to Santry Lane, before heading on towards Coolock. His mother, sitting in the front passenger seat, commented to him about the three 'aircraft' that were straight ahead of them, with their landing lights on. They both presumed that the three bright lights – which were over the Howth area – were aircraft being 'stacked' before approaching Dublin Airport. However, one of these 'aircraft' suddenly shot off northwards, disappearing from sight in only one to two seconds.[23]

Over time, we have discovered that the closer one gets to megalithic sites – such as Tara or Newgrange in the heart of County Meath – the more peculiar such events have been. None have been more bizarre, perhaps, than that which involved the sighting of a colossal object flying slowly over the Manorlands district of the town of Trim, in County Meath. Jimmy Peppard, a town councillor at the time, was at home at about 11.30 p.m. on 8 August 2008, when he received a phone call from his wife, Mary, urging him to go outside and look up. At the time, she was collecting the couple's two teenage sons from a friend's home in the Kildalkey Road area nearby, when one of their sons noticed an object descending from the clouds. Jimmy Peppard later referred to the object as moving 'like a ship through water'. The view of the phenomenon from outside his home was more restricted than at the Kildalkey Road vantage point, but he could make out an 'enormous' outline of the object. He said that it was a 'massive disc' and looked to be at least a mile in diameter and perhaps 3,000 feet (914 metres) up in the air. It had a very bright, flickering light underneath it. He thought that it might have been observing or mapping something on the ground. It passed slowly overhead, and having been visible for around an hour, it drifted towards Summerhill, another town in the area.[24]

Jimmy Peppard later retired from politics. At the time of this event, though, he would have had a lot to lose by making up such a story. Instead, he spoke very candidly to a newspaper about what he had seen. When asked for an opinion of what it was that he saw, his answer was to the point. 'Well, I'll tell you what it wasn't,' he said, 'it wasn't swamp gas lit up by light from Venus and it certainly wasn't a balloon, nor was it any aircraft I have ever seen before.' He further commented that the UAP he had witnessed was not of this earth.[25]

Another odd sighting occurred in County Meath, this time in Slane. On the night of 9 August 2008, George Rock and his son, Connor, were watching a soccer high-lights show when they noticed, through the window beside their television, a small red glow appearing in the sky. They went outside to look at the object, believing that it was a flare. As they watched, it began to move closer and closer to their position, without dimming or losing altitude, until it stopped abruptly over their home. The red 'light' they had first noticed was now a large, spherical object. Moments after stopping, it did a 90-degree turn and shot across the sky, towards Newgrange. It disappeared behind trees on the horizon in a matter of seconds.[26]

With such strange sightings taking place in County Meath, it seemed as though that area had something of a monopoly on aerial weirdness. This wasn't the case, as an aviator was about to find out.

Also in the summer of 2008, an off-duty commercial pilot had driven to the Howth area of Dublin to indulge his pastime of photography. There was lightning in the air and he made many attempts to capture the actual moment of a forked lightning strike. He was successful in photographing a lightning bolt, but on the resulting image, towards the lower right of the frame, a triangular cluster of diffuse white objects appeared, close to the lightning bolt. What this image captured is a mystery.[27]

Two and a half months after the Dunboyne images were recorded, things had returned to a quiet normality for that town's residents, except for Karen Dolan and her husband. At approximately 2.15 a.m. on 19 October, they were driving home, having attended a charity fund-raising event, when they found themselves facing the unknown. While following the Maynooth to Dunboyne road, they were adjacent to Carton Estate when they noticed a formation of brightly-lit, disc-shaped objects overhead. These 'very large' objects moved in a 'slow, deliberate' manner. The phenomena were all bright orange in colour, made no discernible noise on what was a calm and quiet night, and the seven discs stayed in two formations as they moved across the sky at an estimated altitude of only 200 metres or so (around 656 feet). One formation was triangular, while the other group's four discs constituted a diamond shape.

According to the couple's witness statement, the overall length of the formation was over 150 metres (492 feet). A standard question when talking to a UAP witness, or when asking them to complete a witness form, is to estimate the size of the object (or objects) by comparing the size to that of a thumbnail, or perhaps a 5c or 10c coin when held at arm's length. In this case, such methodology was inadequate, as each of the objects was 'at least' the size of a man's fist.

Needless to say, the Dolans accelerated their vehicle to get away from the area, and Karen Dolan told us the UAPs were flying towards Summerhill – again.[28]

As a part of our research into the paranormal in County Meath, we paid many visits to Trim. On a hunch, we sought out a place where people's experiences involving UAPs (or any other paranormal phenomena for that matter) just *might* be discussed. We found 'The Healing Garden', a holistic centre run by Fiona Loughran. Client confidentiality in such an establishment is of paramount importance of course, but having spoken with her about our research, she agreed to pass our details on to anyone who had already reported unusual experiences to her, or who did so later. Such witnesses could then arrange to see us at a later date if they wished and they would have our contact details for possible future use.

Our visit paid off, and on repeated trips in the years that followed we made use of the premises' private consulting rooms to interview a number of witnesses. While the resulting and fascinating accounts of haunted homes (and businesses) are beyond the scope of this book, stories of strange phenomena appearing in the skies overhead were our main focus. Many of these Trim tales told of unknown objects flitting about the sky and of 'satellites' that suddenly stopped dead in their trajectories before resuming on their flight paths ... or that performed right-angled turns at very high speed without decelerating.

Of particular interest were events dating from decades ago and one account had some very familiar aspects to it. The witness, a man now in his forties, telephoned a life-long friend of his before our interview, to make certain that both of them agreed to their story being told. With his friend's approval, the witness then told of how, when they were both twelve years old and playing soccer outside one of their childhood homes, they became aware of a disc-shaped craft approaching. They could clearly see portholes on the object, as it was a bright summer's evening. The two friends stood in awe, rather than fear, as the object hovered only yards away from them, and at a very low altitude. After a short time (or what seemed to them to be a short time), the craft began to accelerate away into the sky. In a few moments, they lost sight of it behind some distant trees. Before the object picked up speed and moved away, it fired a thin beam of light. What's more, the object directed the light not towards the ground, but almost horizontally instead, towards Summerhill. So, the 'beam' phenomenon is far from being a recent development.

Many of the negativists in the Dunboyne case said that a flaw within the digital camera's software was the cause. However, here was a beam, seen by two people, many years before the advent of anything like a modern digital camera – and they saw it without using *any* cameras at all. So such unidentified aerial devices have been firing beams of light for decades, at least, and it *is* possible that these beams can be seen with the naked eye.[29]

A UAP was filmed as it fired red and white beams towards the ground in the Bristol suburb of Dundry, UK. Mother and daughter, Betty and Shellie Williams, watched the spectacle for up to two hours, and used their phones to record footage of the object – or objects, possibly, as two and sometimes three bright aerial objects were seen – as several red and white beams were emitted.

The Avon and Somerset Police said that its helicopter was not airborne in the area at that time, while Bristol Airport's air traffic control said it hadn't received any unusual reports. The witnesses didn't know what might have attracted the attention of a device or craft from who-knows-where, but in daylight they pinpointed the location of the object(s) as having been close to a radio mast at Dundry Hill. A neighbour, Tony Jefferies, commented that he had been observing unusual phenomena in the sky for the previous fortnight.[30]

Yet another 'beam' incident captured on a camera phone involved Zoe Salthouse, a student nurse from New Moston, Manchester, UK. She was sitting with friends one night when she noticed a bright object in the sky. She described its presence as 'eerie and strange' and began recording it on her phone. Suddenly, the object fired a shaft of white light at the ground before disappearing. The shaken student was at a loss to explain what she had seen and recorded, but stated that it didn't look like anything that she had ever seen before.[31] Further recordings of UAP firing beams have since come to public attention, from locations as diverse as Germany, Turkey and the UK.

Of course, we live in an era where Photoshop and similar software applications are commonplace, and where computer-generated imagery (CGI) can create stunning renditions of exotic spaceships for TV and film entertainment. That such technology would spill over into the deliberate hoaxing of UAP was inevitable. However, what about the times before such technology existed and when reports of these things firing beams came from official sources?

One such incident, according to Ministry of Defence files released in the UK, concerned a teenage boy living in Widnes, Cheshire, UK, who found himself being followed by a yellowish-coloured object overhead as he was walking home one night (no date or time recorded for this event). The object, obviously a craft of some sort, was emanating a high-pitched whining noise and was only slightly above rooftop height. It then began to fire beams towards the ground. The terrified youngster ran to his home and blurted out to his father what he had seen. The police were called and they retraced the boy's route home. As a result of their search, four smouldering railway sleepers (ties) were found. One of them had a four-inch-wide hole burned right through it. No traces of petrol or any other accelerant were detected.

MILITARY MATTERS

US Air Force personnel based at the RAF Woodbridge and Bentwaters twin bases in eastern England reported nightly visitations by an aerial intruder in December 1980. This episode – the Rendlesham Forest affair – has been the subject of a considerable amount of investigation and debate. Of interest to us, though, were comments made by former United States Air Force sergeant Larry Warren, who was based there.

In May 2001, American researcher Dr Steven Greer put his Disclosure Project on the world stage at the National Press Club in Washington, DC, and a number of former aerospace, intelligence and military personnel made statements to the assembled media about what they had learned or experienced of unidentified airborne craft over several decades. Larry Warren outlined, briefly, the details of what had occurred at his base in late 1980. He stated that not only were nuclear weapons kept on site – which British people had not been told about – but that an unknown craft was seen over the weapons storage area, firing thin beams of light down at where the warheads were secured.[32]

The interest shown by these objects in nuclear weapons was nothing new, with missiles being rendered unusable while UAP were present at USAF bases in the United States as long ago as the 1960s. The presence of unidentified aerial phenomena emitting *any* sort of beam at a sensitive military site is obviously of concern. This was also the case at a Soviet army weapons depot in the Kasputin Yar district. On the night of 28–29 July 1989, staff at the base's signals centre reported three aerial unknowns. A fighter jet was scrambled to investigate one of these, but it couldn't get close enough to ascertain any details: apparently, the jet was not technologically capable of closing in on the targeted object.

One witness, a Private Bashev, stated that, as one of them flew towards him and others, it divided itself in three and assumed the shape of a triangle. The communications officer on duty, Valery Voloshin, observed the object for two hours. He described it as having a powerful, blinking light, which reminded him of a camera flash lighting up the night sky. He watched as it flew over his unit's logistics yard and on to the base's rocket storage depot, 300 yards (274 metres) away. Its hull gave off a dim green glow. The 4- or 5-metre-wide (13–16 feet wide) object had a semi-spherical, domed top, and from the point where the flashing light had emanated there appeared a beam of light. For several seconds, the beam swept about, illuminating the corner of a building on the base. The intelligently controlled (or piloted) object then drifted away to a nearby railway station, where it again hovered. It then returned to the weapons depot and hovered for a time at an altitude of approximately 197–230 feet (60–70 metres).[33]

The presence of unidentified airborne objects in the supposedly regulated and monitored skies in any country's airspace is disturbing enough, but more troubling still is the problem of unknown craft firing beams – potentially weapons – in that same airspace. Worst of all, though, must be where unusual phenomena or unknown 'aircraft' are involved in a tragedy where the lives of dozens of people are lost and after which certain uncomfortable facts are kept out of the public eye.

3

MYSTERY AT TUSKAR ROCK

From the tasking of a law enforcement aircraft to investigate an unidentified flying object over Dublin, to unknown airborne objects firing beams of light at the ground in Ireland and elsewhere, it might at first appear that aerial mysteries of one kind or another constitute a relatively recent phenomenon in Ireland's skies. Nothing could be further from the truth, however, with some puzzling aspects also featuring in incidents from several decades ago. One such event was the tragic Tuskar Rock air crash, off the country's south-east coast in the 1960s.

FINAL FLIGHT

At 10:32 a.m. GMT (11.32 local time) on 24 March 1968, Flight 712, an Aer Lingus Vickers Viscount 803 aircraft, registration EI-AOM and named *St. Phelim*, took off from Cork Airport en route to London. Thirty-five-year-old Bernard O'Beirne, an experienced pilot who had clocked up 6,683 flying hours during a three-year stint in the Irish military and then with Aer Lingus since 1956, was the captain of Flight 712. Almost 1,700 of his flying hours had been spent on Viscounts. His first officer was Paul Heffernan, who, at twenty-two, had already clocked up 1,139 flying hours, with 900 of them on board the same type of aircraft.[1]

The weather that Sunday morning was good for flying. The Irish government's investigation report on the crash, which was published in the summer of 1970 through the Department of Transport and Power, indicated that no aircraft flying that morning had reported any problematic meteorological conditions. There was a slightly unstable south-south-westerly air flow at all levels, but severe turbulence along the Viscount's planned route was a 'very unlikely' possibility, while the chances of thunderstorms being encountered by the aircraft were deemed to be 'probably virtually nil' in the report's summary of the weather conditions that morning.

As the propellers on the aircraft began to spin, and as its four Rolls-Royce engines roared and lifted the sixty-one people on board into the sky to begin their 100-minute routine flight, little did anyone know that within half that time all of them would be dead. What happened to the aircraft, and what caused it to plummet into the sea off the coast of County Wexford, are factors that have remained both mysterious and controversial for more than four decades. Further confusion has been added by the use of both GMT and local time in documentation relating to the case. The principal focus, though, is centred on what happened in a crucial period of forty-five minutes or so from the aircraft taking off until its demise.

The Tuskar Rock incident has produced a huge amount of material from the worlds of both officialdom and investigative journalism. The sequence of events during the flight, garnered largely from the radio transmissions between EI-AOM and the ground, and subsequently reproduced in official documentation, has been examined thoroughly by journalists and aviation experts alike over the years.

The views of Michael O'Toole in *Cleared For Disaster* (2006) and Dermot Walsh in *Tragedy at Tuskar Rock* (1983) provide an illuminating insight into the sequence of events on that March morning. However, a study of the 1970 official report is also necessary, to build up a more complete picture of what unfolded and of what the Irish government has had to say about the incident, both then and now. A study of all three documents leaves no doubt that highly unusual aspects of the crash still remain troubling. The public still does not know the whole story of what happened on that day. Perhaps it never will.

There were four official probes into the Tuskar Rock incident. The Irish government's 1970 report was later followed by the undertaking of two reviews of all of the relevant data and files between 1998 and 2002, both of which were set in motion by the minister with responsibility for transport at the time, Mary O'Rourke. Following the disaster, Aer Lingus also conducted its own internal investigation. Yet despite all of this, many disturbing questions remain.

Just what *did* happen to Flight 712? A summary of the Viscount's last moments, according to the 'History of the Flight' section of the 1970 Irish government report is given below.

A few minutes after it took off from Cork Airport, the *St. Phelim* had cleared 7,000 feet (2,134 metres). At 10.38 a.m. the aircraft was instructed that it had clearance to proceed to Tuskar Rock. The planned route for the flight involved the Viscount flying along the country's south coast, heading via the Tuskar Rock to Strumble Head in south-west Wales.

Two minutes later, the Viscount radioed that it was close to Youghal, had reached an altitude of 7,500 feet (2,286 metres) and was climbing up to 17,000 feet (5,182 metres). Cork ATC then suggested that, if its pilots wished, it could route directly to Strumble. No direct acceptance of this suggestion was received in response.

At 10.57:07 a.m. a radio transmission from the Viscount stated that it was now 'by Bannow [an aircraft reporting point over the sea, west of Strumble], level 170 [17,000 feet/5,182 metres], estimating Strumble at 03'. With the aircraft thus due to arrive at Strumble within the next six minutes – at three minutes past the hour – the flight was then instructed to change its radio frequency to 131.2 MHz, so that it could communicate with London Airways. The reply of '131.2' came from the aircraft, with the time now recorded at 10.57:29 a.m.

London radar picked up a message at 10.58:02 a.m. from the Aer Lingus aircraft: 'Echo India Alpha Oscar Mike with you.' The signal was garbled, as it was simultaneous with another call. Just eight seconds later, London received a further contact from EI-AOM. This transmission was also received by another Aer Lingus Viscount, flying from Dublin to Bristol as Flight EI 362, and by a BOAC aircraft, Flight 506. The message, which was difficult to distinguish amid a lot of background noise on the recording, was later interpreted by some listeners as '5,000 feet descending, spinning rapidly'. These were the last words that anyone heard from the aircraft.

According to the 'Consideration of Probabilities' section of the Irish government's report, compiled by R. W. O'Sullivan, inspector of air accidents, the aircraft's height was not 5,000 feet (1,524 metres) after all. Instead, it was 12,000 feet (3,658 metres). The higher figure was settled on following intensive examination of the recording carried out by the Civil Aeronautics Board (CAB), the Institute for Industrial Research & Standards (IIRS) and the Federal Bureau of Investigation (FBI).

The technical analysis and expertise of the day concluded that 12,000 feet (3,658 metres) *must* have been the aircraft's altitude at this point, as it had been cruising at 17,000 feet (5,182 metres) as recently as 10.57:07 a.m., when it reported its position as being close to Bannow. The distorted radio message came just eight seconds after the 'Echo India Alpha Oscar Mike' communication. If the 5,000 feet (1,524 metres) altitude interpretation had been correct, then the 12,000-foot (3,658-metre) drop in height – from 17,000 feet (5,182 metres) eight seconds earlier – would have meant that the vertical component of velocity would need to have been 1,500 feet (457 metres) per second. O'Sullivan's report stated that this was 'quite an impossible speed for this aircraft to have attained'.

The report also points out that, even if the aircraft had begun to descend from 17,000 feet (5,182 metres) just after its 10.57:07 a.m. (Bannow) radio message, then it would have descended 12,000 feet (3,658 metres) to 5,000 feet (1,524 metres) in forty-one seconds, a vertical velocity component of 200 miles (322 km) per hour, a prospect that was 'not considered feasible', according to the report. As a passenger aircraft moves from one altitude to another, it is a gradual process. A descent like this could not have happened so quickly, as the aircraft would have disintegrated in mid-air due to the extreme forces acting upon the airframe.

On the basis that neither of the above scenarios would be probable – let alone possible, O'Sullivan concluded that the interpreted height of 12,000 feet (3,658 metres) in the final transmission, rather than 5,000 feet (1,524 metres), was 'much more likely' to have been correct. Yet only four lines in the report's 'Consideration of Probabilities' section are then given to looking at the alternative: that if the figure of 12,000 feet (3,658 metres) was correct, then the *St. Phelim* would still have lost 5,000 feet (1,524 metres) in altitude in just eight seconds. That works out at 37,500 feet (11,430 metres) per minute … a figure that was 'not considered possible' in O'Sullivan's conclusions. If 5,000 feet

(1,524 metres) in altitude was lost in the forty-one seconds, then the average descent rate would have been 7,320 feet (2,231 metres) per minute.

The calculation of the rate of descent over a minute by O'Sullivan distracts from the fact that, over a much shorter period of time, the aircraft evidently lost an incredible amount of height, without disintegrating. With the lack of any information from flight recorders – the aircraft wasn't carrying any such equipment – this altitude puzzle, and the message from 10.57 given under apparently normal conditions, remain.

At 11.10 a.m. London ATC contacted its counterparts at Shannon, County Clare, in the west of Ireland, to advise them that there was no further radio link with the *St. Phelim*. Three minutes later, London informed Shannon that it had asked the Aer Lingus Dublin to Bristol flight (EI 362) to search for the missing aircraft west of Strumble. The aircraft did as requested, descending to just 500 feet (152 metres) in good visibility to look for the lost aircraft, but found nothing.

At 11.25 a.m., following more than ten minutes of further attempts to make radio contact with the missing Viscount, a full alert was declared. Nothing was found that day, but by 1.10 p.m. the United Kingdom had ten aircraft searching for wreckage. An initial report from the UK authorities to the Irish Naval Service base at Haulbowline, County Cork, suggested that debris had been sighted floating at geographical coordinates 51:57N, 06:10W, off the south-eastern coast of Ireland. Two ships within 4 nautical

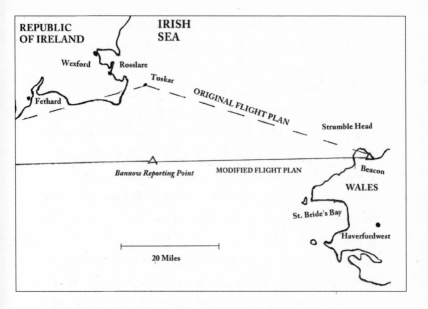

REPUBLIC OF IRELAND

IRISH SEA

Wexford

Rosslare

Tuskar

ORIGINAL FLIGHT PLAN

Strumble Head

Fethard

Bannow Reporting Point   MODIFIED FLIGHT PLAN

Beacon

WALES

St. Bride's Bay

Haverfordwest

20 Miles

miles of the site saw nothing, however. Nor did the Rosslare lifeboat. At 12.52 p.m. the Irish Air Corps stated that it had sent a Dove aircraft and a helicopter to conduct a search, but at 3.30 p.m. the report of floating debris being sighted was cancelled.

At 6.15 a.m. the next morning, British ships and aircraft resumed their search and at 12.41 p.m. wreckage was found and bodies recovered at a location 6 nautical miles north-east of Tuskar Rock. The Irish naval vessel, the LE *Macha*, joined the operation on 26 March as Search Controller, having halted its patrol duties off Ireland's north-west coast. Thirteen bodies were found in the following days, as well as floating debris. Some time later, a fourteenth body was discovered. The location of the bulk of the wreckage couldn't be pinpointed, despite the deployment of sonar on Royal Navy ships and trawling by the Irish fishing vessels *Glendalough* and *Cú na Mara*. Finally, on 5 and 6 June, 1.72 nautical miles from Tuskar Rock, with Tuskar Rock bearing 280 degrees, in 39 fathoms, both trawlers succeeded in locating wreckage. Divers from the Royal Navy ship HMS *Reclaim* confirmed that there was a mass of debris on the seabed.

Salvage operations following this discovery of wreckage confirmed that at least 'a major portion' of the aircraft had been located. The line of sight of two eyewitnesses – one a sailor on board a vessel in the area, and the other on shore, near Greenore Point – coincided with the area in which the debris was found. Both had seen something splashing into the water there and placed the time of their sightings as between 11.10 a.m. and 11.15 a.m. Some more wreckage was found by the *Glendalough*, captained by Billy Bates, a year and a half after the tragedy.

After a visual inspection on recovery, the pieces of wreckage were transported on Irish Army vehicles to the Air Corps' headquarters at Casement Aerodrome, Baldonnel, County Dublin. There, they were reassembled on a timber frame in a hangar. The aircraft's components were inspected and then examined at their manufacturers' works.

Several months after the crash, a portion of the elevator spring tab from the Viscount's port elevator was found on a beach between Rosslare Harbour and Greenore Point, 7 miles west of where the main body of wreckage was located. This item could not float. It was tangled in seaweed, which

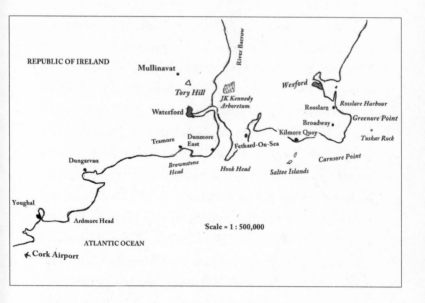

was not prevalent in the area where the bulk of the debris was found. It could, therefore, have detached from the aircraft before the crash, and become caught up in the seaweed closer to land. Rough weather could then have brought it ashore.

In the 'Tests and Research' section of the 1970 investigation report, items (i) to (v) detail the technical analysis carried out on the pieces of located debris. Of note is the fact that the manufacturers' examination of all of the recovered engine and propeller parts indicated damage that was consistent with a sudden and violent impact with the sea, with no evidence of any pre-impact defect or damage. This would seem to rule out a bird-strike on one or more of the engines as a cause of the crash. Such an occurrence was apparently suggested as a cause, especially since, according to Michael O'Toole's analysis of the incident, Bewick's or Whooper swans had almost caused an air accident in the winter of 1967–8. The birds were flying at record heights in the Outer Hebrides islands area when this incident happened. The 1970 report's 'Analysis and Conclusions' section (part vi) also casts doubt on the bird-strike theory. It cites expert opinion that, while the presence of large migratory birds would not be an unfamiliar sight in south-eastern Ireland, it would be highly unlikely that they would reach an altitude of 17,000 feet (5,182 metres). This opinion also surmised that flights of migratory birds would rarely occur in daytime and, the report continued, the good weather up to 24 March that year would have meant that all (or at least most) of these large birds would already have left the region.

The report states that while there were twenty-nine witnesses to the catastrophe, only two of these actually saw the moment of the aircraft's impact with the sea – the sailor and the person on shore mentioned earlier. In the compilation of the report, therefore, their sightings put the actual time of the crash at between 11.10 a.m. and 11.15 a.m., as these were the times given by these eyewitnesses. In opting for this time, however, confusion and controversy abound. The report discounts the testimony of several people who had observed unusual events in the sky before that time. In two or three very brief paragraphs, such testimony was discounted. Most of these witnesses were interviewed twice between the time of the crash and the conclusion of the gathering of evidence for the report. In all cases, these people made no changes to their testimony between the interviews, yet R. W. O'Sullivan insisted that the evidence of 'non-expert' witnesses could not be depended on. Even the accuracy of their clocks and watches was called into question, as was their ability to tell the time! When witness testimony included timings that could not readily be explained, all such statements were brushed aside with a comment that country folk had a habit of setting their watches and clocks ahead of everyone else. Their version of events, therefore, could not be relied on … unless, of course, it coincided with the official view. So, phenomena that were heard or seen well before the believed time of impact – and which therefore did not fit into what might be considered an 'acceptable' timeline of events – were simply discounted. The failure of the investigation to engage in such a discussion is summed up in the report as follows: 'whenever evidence on timing appeared to be probably unreliable, it was of course rejected after due consideration of the implications involved'.

What implications are these? What was it that these witnesses heard and saw that could possibly be so unpalatable to an Irish government investigation? Their words have since added even more mystery to an already strange story, but the Tuskar Rock disaster had long since generated a more pressing suggestion that has been repeated and debated ever since: that the doomed aircraft had been struck by a British missile or a target drone, or by another (probably military) aircraft. In 1968, with an increasingly serious political situation unfolding in Northern Ireland, such an occurrence – if it were ever officially confirmed – could very well have had grave consequences for stability and security in both Britain and Ireland.

The investigation report includes in its concluding paragraphs a curious but extremely serious point. R. W. O'Sullivan states that the possibility of 'another aircraft' having been involved in the loss of the *St. Phelim* could not be ruled out. In the last of twelve points which comprise the 'Findings' section, he asserts that 'there is evidence which could be construed as indicative of the possible presence of another aircraft or airborne object in the vicinity'. If this aircraft or object either collided with the Viscount, or flew close enough to it to cause it to make a sudden evasive manoeuvre, or flew past it and caused wake turbulence, then the Aer Lingus aircraft could have entered a fatal spin or spiral dive into the sea.

The report holds back from any further support for this theory, but does finish the point by saying that even though there is 'no substantiating evidence' of this having actually occurred, the possibility 'cannot be excluded for it is compatible with all of the presently available evidence'.

In the absence of data, it took very little for the belief that a cover-up had occurred to take root. The inconclusive nature of the 1970 report contributed greatly to the rumour mill in Ireland that the British (and possibly Irish) authorities were well aware that military activity had resulted in the downing of the Aer Lingus aircraft. Press speculation and rumours circulating among the public echoed each other in

MYSTERY AT TUSKAR ROCK

this regard, with some even accepting it as a 'fact' that a missile, drone, or some other military aircraft, had either collided with the Viscount or caused it to make a fatal evasive
manoeuvre.

A new examination of the incident was required. In 1998
a meeting took place between Veronica Sutherland, the UK's
ambassador to the Republic of Ireland, and the Irish minister with responsibility for transport, Mary O'Rourke. The
year of the thirtieth anniversary of the disaster also saw the
ambassador meeting relatives of those who lost their lives
in the Tuskar Rock crash and she agreed with the minister
that the incident needed to be looked at again. This new
analysis was published in August 2000. The *Review of Irish
and UK Files on the Loss of the Aer Lingus Viscount St. Phelim
Registration EI-AOM on 24 March 1968* was conducted by
Kevin Humphreys, the chief inspector of air accidents at
the Air Accident Investigation Unit (AAIU), and Graham
Liddy, inspector of air accidents with the same unit. This
document reiterates that the height of the aircraft in the
'spinning rapidly' message was, in fact, 12,000 feet (3,658
metres). It also contains a correction of the details of the
route taken by the Viscount in the first few minutes after it
took off from Cork. The original (1970) report had stated
that Cork had made the suggestion to the Viscount that
it could fly further south, if desired, and so take a course
that would include the Bannow reporting point on the way
across the sea towards Strumble. It would actually have been
Shannon that made this suggestion, as the aircraft was flying

through the Shannon Flight Information Region (FIR).
Indeed, Shannon ATC had already been on the telephone
with London Airways to seek clearance for the aircraft to
fly direct from Cork to Strumble. This route would take
the Viscount out over the sea off Ireland's southern coastline. The requested clearance was given and at 10.40 a.m.
this suggested route was duly radioed to the aircraft from
Shannon. The 'History of the Flight' section of the 1970
report was unclear on this point. Dermot Walsh included
the details of Shannon ATC's telephone conversation with
London Airways in his book, *Tragedy at Tuskar Rock*. He
obtained the details from Irish government departmental
files on the case, and states 'the [1970] accident investigation report does not coincide with department appendices
about the exchange of messages about taking the short-cut
to Strumble'.

At this point, it is appropriate to return to the statements by witnesses that were mentioned in the original
government report in 1970, statements which indicated that
the Viscount was nowhere near where it was meant to be
around the time of the crash and which also indicated that
a second, unidentified aircraft or object was in fact flying
over the south-eastern corner of Ireland around the time
of the incident. Both the report and the *Review* follow a
strict protocol of not listing the witnesses by name, opting
instead to allocate them numbers. Again, the use of GMT
in the reviewed files is confusing, but the original government report had opted to use it in listing the order of events,

as seen and heard by these witnesses. For the sake of clarity, GMT is being used in this chapter.

Between 10.55 a.m. and 11.00 a.m., ten witnesses (numbered from eight to twelve and from twenty-two to twenty-six) in the Broadway area heard a loud noise that was compared to a 'very sharp roll' of thunder. One witness further described a double 'clap', like thunder, coming from the direction of Tuskar Rock. At some time between 10.45 a.m. and 11.05 a.m., in the Fethard-on-Sea, County Wexford area, witness No. 2 saw an aircraft partly enveloped in a swirling cloud and then heard a loud sound, like thunder. The aircraft then flew south-east towards the Saltee Islands. The cloud enveloped the plane's nose and a portion of a wing. Between 10.45 a.m. and 11.15 a.m., also in the Fethard-on-Sea vicinity, witness No. 1 saw a plane emerging in a sharp turn from three small black clouds. The aircraft, descending and looking quite unsteady in its flight, looked as if it had been 'fired out' of these clouds, according to the witness, and it then made its way towards the south.

During the same thirty-minute period, four more witnesses in the same area – Nos 3, 3(a), 4 and 4(a) – saw an aircraft with a red colour on its wings and tail. The initial impression they had, because of the bright red colour, was that the aircraft looked as if it was on fire, but there was no smoke trail. It flew towards the south-east.

At 11.02 a.m. two witnesses at Carnsore Point, County Wexford (Nos 13 and 14), heard a bang that sounded like thunder. The first of these witnesses also reported seeing a dark cloud, low down in the sky, between Tuskar and Barrels Rock. Between 11.10 a.m. and 11.15 a.m., witness No. 19 – the sailor on board a passing ship, the MV *Metric*, saw a plane diving into the sea near Tuskar Rock and a column of water being thrown up by the impact. In the same time frame (though the *Review* cites 11.11 a.m. rather than 11.10 a.m. as the earliest time of the witness' experience, as stated in the 1970 report), someone else saw the spouting of water near Tuskar Rock. This witness, No. 17, was near Greenore Point, County Wexford. From that location, a sound 'like water running off rocks' was heard, a fact that was supported by witness No. 18. Their interpretation of the noise was akin to 'stones [being] tipped out of a lorry'.

The sighting of an aircraft with red colouring in the area is troubling. Such paintwork was not consistent with Aer Lingus livery, so this aircraft could not have been the Viscount. Bright 'dayglo' paintwork did, however, feature prominently on Irish military aircraft. Yet no Irish Air Corps aircraft were in the area at that time, with its Dove aircraft not arriving to conduct a search until well after the crash had happened.

The 1970 report points out that there were discrepancies in the descriptions of the sounds heard by these witnesses, but subjective interpretation of noises by individuals should be borne in mind. It is mooted that the 'thunder' sounds may have been akin to a sonic boom. If there *was* a sonic boom, then *what* could have caused it?

The 1970 report concludes that if EI-AOM had already descended in a spin or spiral dive, and if some control of the aircraft had been re-established, then it could have flown westwards until it was over the Fethard-on-Sea area, between 10.45 a.m. and 11.15 a.m. It could then have flown south-east out to sea near Hook Head, County Wexford, then to a location east of Tuskar Rock, before plummeting into the water. If so, the aircraft would have flown over 60 miles between 10.58 a.m. and 11.10 a.m./11.15 a.m. This short time period would have meant the Viscount travelling at 212 miles (341 km) per hour. This would not be impossible, according to the report's text, but it would have been 'extremely unlikely' if the aircraft was by then in a damaged or disabled state.

If the Viscount was not seen in the south County Wexford region, then the puzzles remain of just who was piloting (or operating) the aircraft with the red paintwork and what kind of aircraft – or device – it actually was. Also, the 1970 report did not account satisfactorily for the strange booms that were heard, or the small clouds that were seen with the unidentified aircraft. The idea is put forward that the description of the clouds around the aircraft sounded like condensation being caused by a supersonic aircraft coming out of a dive through humid air. The prospect of an aircraft or some other aerial object possibly capable of flying at supersonic speed is mentioned again, yet no explanation is offered as to what type of aircraft this could have been, or who was flying it.

Questions by the press and by members of the general public concerning the UK's test-firing of surface-to-air munitions in the south Irish Sea area in 1968 have been raised periodically over the last four decades, with the focus of some observers falling not just on the test ranges in Wales, but on the involvement of two Royal Navy ships in the incident. Britain's MoD, in response to queries, has repeatedly stated that HMS *Hardy* and HMS *Penelope* were not equipped with surface-to-air missiles, and that the vessels' involvement, after the crash, was to assist in the search for debris.

The suspicion of a missile or target drone having been in the skies over south County Wexford was fuelled in no small part by the witness testimony of two people. At Hook Head, south of Fethard-on-Sea, witness No. 6 observed an object in the sea on the afternoon of the crash, near the Coningmore Half Tide Rock. Witness No. 7, from Newtown, north of Fethard-on-Sea, also saw this unidentified object. The latter witness noticed a ship passing by, between the floating object and the shore, but the vessel didn't alter course to investigate. The witness thought no more of it at the time and nothing was found in the area in a later search.

The original Irish government probe offers a 'remote possibility' as to what happened on that terrible March day. When EI-AOM was within six minutes' flying time of Strumble Head, it was upset or struck by another aircraft of some sort. This unidentified flying object – which is what such an 'aircraft' would have been – caused the Viscount to go into a spin or a spiral dive. It recovered sufficiently to fly for another ten minutes or so, until control was irretrievably lost. In this scenario, the unidentified flying object which may have triggered this horrific sequence of events, might have been what the witnesses in the Fethard-on-Sea area observed, and it then crashed into the sea near the Saltee Islands. (Further reading of the official documentation on the witnesses' accounts reveals that the object seen floating there was a 'metallic' colour.)

This possibility is countered by the investigator's insistence that some other key factors needed to be considered. The first of these was that the altitude of 17,000 feet (5,182 metres) was deemed to be an unlikely height at which military activity would have been conducted. Also, no civil or military aircraft, either piloted or unmanned, were reported missing by the British (or Irish) authorities on the date of the crash. He then reiterates that the British missile ranges in Wales were closed that day and that there were no aircraft carriers operating in the area at the relevant time.

The *Review* published in 2000 followed in the footsteps of the original 1970 investigation report by focusing largely on complex technical matters concerning the aircraft itself. Both of the reports looked in detail at the possibility of a catastrophic mechanical failure having caused the Viscount to break up in mid-air, though this idea could not be strongly supported, as the tail section has never been found. The conclusions in 2000 stated that the later finding of the elevator spring tab on a beach was an indication that the plane may not have been fully intact when it hit the water. Furthermore, the *Review* said that the eventual discovery of pieces of missile-related debris in that area of the sea by trawlers, or washed up on shore – from such objects as Jindivik, Meteor and Stiletto target drones – were not connected to the crash. Also, any query in the public's mind as to why the British authorities began their search for the crashed aircraft so far away from where the two eyewitnesses saw it hitting the water near Tuskar Rock was addressed by stating that all the Royal Navy initially had to go on was the Viscount's last known position on its journey towards Wales, which was past Bannow. As the aircraft was understood to be in the London Flight Information Region (FIR) when it went down, international agreements meant that the British military was obliged to use its resources to help in the search operation.

The problem is that the 2000 *Review*, by restricting itself to the same parameters as its predecessor thirty years earlier, sidestepped some witness testimony that did not make sense to those conducting the original investigation. After all, the 1970 report mentioned that there were twenty-nine witnesses, yet not all of these were discussed within its pages. Only 'a small number' of new witnesses were interviewed for the 2000 version, with two of these, who both saw the Viscount taking off in Cork, commenting that the aircraft didn't look 'normal' as it gained altitude. There is no elaboration on this. Nor is there any discussion of an account given by a third new witness who, aged twelve or thirteen at the time, saw a large aircraft approaching him in the Tory Hill area of south County Wexford, as he tended livestock in fields. The aircraft turned right, gained altitude as it flew out to sea, and it then plummeted into the water. The time of this event was put at about eleven o'clock (midday local). By this time, however, the aircraft would have already reported its Bannow position and would not have been near where the witness was located, and would, instead, have been flying between Bannow and Strumble.

Similarly, the *Review of Irish and UK Files* acknowledges the multi-witness sighting of an aircraft with reddish colouring over south County Wexford, but it fails to discuss the matter any further. Instead, it states that the link between an aircraft at Fethard-on-Sea going in a south or south-east direction with the Viscount spinning at 10.58 a.m., 'twenty miles away', is 'very tenuous'.

The *Review of Irish and UK Files* also did not discuss what witness No. 5 had stated to the original investigation: he or she had heard an undefined 'noise' between Slade and the Coningbeg lighthouse. The sound faded away, but three or four minutes later another, louder one was heard which lasted about two minutes and seemed to be coming from the sky. It stopped abruptly, with the witness judging that it had emanated from somewhere between Slade and the Saltee Islands. All of this happened between approximately 10.40 a.m. and 10:45/10.50 a.m. What could this have been, so long before there was any indication that something was wrong with the aircraft?

The lack of any definitive answers in the 1970 report continued with the *Review*'s assessment of the British and

Irish authorities' files in 2000. On page 64, it states that no tape recordings of the radio exchanges between the Viscount and the Irish ATC units could be located. This frustrating fact was compounded by another: the disappearance of log books belonging to some of the British ships in the area of the crash on that March day. Despite some conjecture that several such logs had rather curiously vanished, the MoD told the *Review* that just two had been mislaid – those of HMS *Hardy* and HMS *Clarbeston*. The logs of all the other Royal Navy ships involved were available for study at the UK National Archives at Kew, Greater London, or they would otherwise become available under the provisions of the thirty-year rule. Administrative error was cited as a possible explanation for the disappearance of the two log books. The *Clarbeston* was retired in December 1968, when its logs should have been archived, but the correct procedure for doing so was apparently not followed. The *Hardy*, meanwhile, was refitted in Gibraltar in May of the same year. Its logs may have been mislaid during this period.

In early February 2000, the AAIU team interviewed Captain P. G. McCabe, who had been involved in the Irish government's 1970 investigation. He said he had always been puzzled over how the elevator spring tab was found so far from the site of the main wreckage and he remained curious as to what was seen flying over the southern part of County Wexford close to the time of the crash. According to McCabe, something was observed flying as low as just 200 feet (61 metres) over the Saltee Islands area and he remarked that the British military had failed to investigate this sighting promptly, where the floating object had subsequently been seen. (He told the *Review* that the British authorities had cited dangerous conditions there as a reason for this.) He also informed the AAIU team that, within days of the crash, he and his colleagues had amassed almost *fifty* statements from witnesses – not just twenty-nine, which the resulting official report had mentioned – telling them about something else having been seen in the sky. This unidentified phenomenon was very definitely *not* the doomed Viscount.

The Tuskar Rock incident had attracted the attention of the Celtic League, a group which represents the interests of Celtic people in Ireland, Britain, the Isle of Man and France. It involved itself in the search for answers in the Tuskar Rock case and put a series of questions to the MoD, as did a committee representing relatives of those killed in the crash. The relatives also put a list of queries to the Irish government. Both governments gave answers, and the *Review* contains a lengthy examination of these exchanges in its contents.

One of the first questions asked of the Irish authorities concerned the dearth of relevant logs or papers in the possession of the UK authorities. The query referred to records that had 'gone missing' or that had 'disappeared' or been 'shredded' since the disaster. After more than thirty years, the Irish authorities' reply was, simply, that this question should be addressed instead to the UK authorities!

This set the tone for some more unusual answers. The Irish authorities were asked why it was that an American man named as 'Walcott', an air accident investigator, was prevented from working with the relatives in the early 1970s. The short (and solitary) response was that an attempt would be made to ascertain if any record could be found of Walcott.

Given the resources of the Irish government, this ought to have been quite a simple matter to clear up, yet it had not been done by the time the *Review* was published. Checks could have been carried out, presumably, with the archive sections of such agencies as the Federal Aviation Administration (FAA) and the National Transportation Safety Board (NTSB). If Walcott had been a serving or retired American investigator at that time, then the FAA or the NTSB should have been able to furnish more details to the Irish authorities while the *Review* was ongoing.

Readers will probably be familiar with the 'men in black' (MIB) phenomenon. Basically, this involves the frequently bizarre interrogation of those who claim to have had UAP sightings or experiences, by strange-looking or oddly-behaving visitors. It is not our assertion that such inquisitive (and uninvited) MIBs are necessarily extraterrestrial in origin. Indeed, the three men who paid a visit to one alarmed young witness to the Tuskar Rock incident *seemed* all too human. On the Wednesday following the crash, witness Martin Connelly was disturbed at school by the unknown visitors. Taken out of his classroom, he was told that 'he saw nothing' on the day of the disaster. One of the men appeared to be British, while his two colleagues spoke with Irish accents.

The response of the *Review* to this revelation was muted – and it also succeeded in missing the point completely. The visit to the boy's school was, the Irish authorities replied, 'to fully verify his statements and the records show that the Royal Navy commented that he was very accurate'. It went on to state that the information that he gave 'contributed in a large way to the discovery of the wreckage', but did not address the core issue of an alleged attempt being made to persuade a witness to stay silent.

Another disturbing prospect arose: why was it, the Irish authorities were asked, that an Irish Naval Service officer told the skipper of the trawler *Glendalough*, Billy Bates, that if any body parts were found they were to be thrown back into the sea? The answer that was given was that the naval officer now disputed this and that it was (then) currently the subject of legal proceedings. Bates made the assertion, again, over three decades after the event, in testimony he gave at Kilmore Quay on 14 February 1999.

Our analysis of the Tuskar Rock crash has, so far, focused on the first two investigations, published by the Irish government in 1970 and again thirty years later, in 2000. Despite the considerable efforts made by the investigators to put together both reports, these probes left many key questions unanswered. Yet another official inquiry into the incident was needed, and the Irish minister with responsibility for transport, Mary O'Rourke, commissioned this in the summer of 2000, just weeks before the *Review* was completed and made available.

Undoubtedly, the hope was that this third examination of the case would finally put an end to the many mysteries that had gone unsolved in the first two – and, at the same time, stifle the various conspiracy theories about the crash that had grown during the previous thirty-two years. Indeed, the thirtieth anniversary of the crash was marked by the transmission, by state broadcaster RTÉ, of a *Prime Time* television documentary focusing on the missile theory.

However, any such hope for the new probe – which was completed in November 2001 and had appendices, annexes and comments added to its text the following January – was to be short-lived.

4

TUSKAR ROCK – CASE UNSOLVED

The third probe was undertaken, not by members of the country's air accident investigation staff, but by an international team of aviation experts. The team was to produce a very lengthy study contained in three bulky volumes, one of which was subdivided into three tomes. In total, the huge file of investigative documentation supplied to Dermot Butler by the Irish government in relation to this incident weighed in at well over 7 pounds (3 kilograms), comprising the international team's study, the *Review of Irish and UK Files* that came before it and the full version of the 1970 report. (The shortened version that was originally made available to the public was just over twenty pages long.)

The team given the unenviable task of trying to shed further light on the Tuskar Rock puzzle was made up of three members: Colin Torkington, Yves Lemercier and Manuel Pech. Colin Torkington had a Master of Science degree in aeronautical engineering and he began his career with the

Vickers-Armstrong company in the UK in 1952. He held a private pilot's licence and a glider qualification, and on moving to Australia in 1961 he joined the Department of Civil Aviation as an airworthiness engineer. A Fellow of the Royal Aeronautical Society, he had worked on several major accident investigations, two of which involved Viscount aircraft that suffered structural failure in flight. He became Head of Airworthiness in the Australian Civil Aviation Authority and had written no fewer than twenty-five papers, seventeen of which had been published.

Yves Lemercier logged over 7,000 flight hours in fifteen aircraft types in the French military as a captain, a squadron leader and as a training operations safety manager. Finally retiring with the rank of Rear Admiral, he joined the French equivalent of the NTSB, the BEA (Bureau Enquettes-Accidents). Having subsequently taken part in many air crash investigations in France and elsewhere, he was made principal officer in charge of dealing with accidents and the investigation of serious incidents.

Manuel Pech served in the French navy from 1954 to 1981. During his military career, he spent five years flight-testing aircraft and a further six years as a captain of a maritime patrol crew. As a crew captain he clocked up 3,500 flight hours on ten types of aircraft operated by the navy. From his retirement in 1981 up to the time of the study being conducted on the Tuskar Rock incident, he had worked on programmes for the helicopter division of Aerospatiale (later Eurocopter).

The vast knowledge and experience of all three were beyond doubt. However, the first page of the team's resulting report indicated that nothing had really changed. The preface clearly stated that the study 'does not constitute a formal investigation' of the incident. Rather, its function was 'to shed further light, if possible, on the cause or causes of the accident'.

In effect, the 1970 investigation report was inconclusive and the later *Review of Irish and UK Files* was similarly impaired, relying so much on the original. And now, the opening page of the study by the international team was as good as telling the reader that it, in turn, would primarily be re-examining both of the earlier works. It was readily apparent that, as far as the quest for final and definitive answers was concerned, this seemed to be little more than officialdom's way of simply rearranging the deckchairs on board the *Titanic*.

The international team's study looked again at the idea that a bird-strike might have caused the Viscount to lose control and crash. Referring to data from the Wildfowl and Wetlands Trust (WWT), the team referred to the original bird migration patterns for early 1968. The WWT information suggested to the team that, with Whooper swans flying up towards Iceland and their Bewick cousins making their way over towards Siberia, their migratory flight paths would cross each other between south-east Wexford and the south-west coast of Wales. The team referred again to the altitude record for migratory swans – which it put at 25,400 feet (7,468 metres), which had been observed in the Outer Hebrides area during the previous December. It noted that a 'potential collision course' would have existed along the Viscount's route. The renewed issue of a bird-strike is strange, to say the least, considering that the 1970 report clearly stated that there was no indication of damage to the aircraft's propellers or engines prior to impact with the sea.

The chain of evidence was only as strong as its weakest link, and while the international team had set about its task in an enthusiastic manner, some serious shortcomings soon became apparent in what it had to work with. It stated that a 'source of inaccuracy' existed in the fact that it was not clear when, precisely, the aircraft left the original route, via Tuskar, and opted instead to fly directly to Strumble. This is true, but the fact of the matter was that the 'by Bannow' message had been broadcast *before* there was any indication that anything was wrong with the aircraft. This position put the flight miles away from where so many witnesses reported seeing it – and miles away from where so many witnesses reported seeing *something else* flying around the skies of southern County Wexford.

The study referred to 'several statements' that 'had to be rejected' in the earlier investigative efforts. For the most part, such statements were made by witnesses who were situated west of Waterford and by those witnesses who had 'positively identified an Aer Lingus Viscount, flying (at an abnormal altitude) over Old Parish, or Ballykelly'. The words of one witness, though, about what he observed at

Hook Head, were considered reliable … yet the same witness was not deemed credible for seeing something else in the Ballykelly area.

Whatever this witness reported in his two accounts, just one of them was believed in the earlier probes. This is an indication that certain sightings were seemingly discounted on the basis that they just *couldn't* be true in the eyes of officialdom, even if the witnesses were being completely honest in what they said they had observed. There was no mention of anyone on the original investigation team going to interview those witnesses whose accounts were not recorded.

Yet another puzzling weakness in the international team's evaluation of the case centres on the mysterious airborne object that was reported flying over the general Fethard-on-Sea area. Its conclusion was that – presumably having reviewed what the MoD had said before about the lack of UK military activity in the area – such an 'air mobile' in that place at that time 'cannot be a missile or a drone having "collided" or "near collided" with the Viscount'. So, the possibility of *something else* being in the sky in the area still existed, but this was not pursued.

The international team looked at an aspect of the disaster that had perplexed many observers during the previous years: the lack of radio traffic between the aircraft and the ground, particularly if, as had been postulated, the Viscount was flying for some time in a disabled condition before it finally crashed. The *Review* had produced documentation showing that the interference on the aircraft's message just

after 10.58 a.m. may have been caused by radio signals emanating from a Territorial Army exercise taking place at the
time. However, such land-based activity by British reservist
troops was not the main issue. Of more immediate importance was the radio silence from the Viscount in its final
minutes, with questions having been raised concerning
whether the aircraft's radio had been too badly damaged
in a mid-air collision – an unlikely prospect, as it had then
managed to transmit the 'by Bannow', 'with you' and 'spinning rapidly' messages – or whether its frequency couldn't
be received at ground stations from certain altitudes and so
on.

In response to this complex issue, the team conducted
an analysis of the 'radio propagation aspects' in the case and
concluded that the 'spinning rapidly' message was sent when
the aircraft was, in fact, at just 5,000 feet (1,524 metres) in
altitude (even though the 1970 report stated categorically
that this would have been impossible). Furthermore, given
the locations of *all* the witnesses, and the times of their
sightings of the Viscount, the chilling message would have
been sent not after the Bannow reporting point had been
left behind, but in the area of the Kennedy Arboretum in
south County Wexford.

The team decided to retrace what they believed to be
the Viscount's final journey, by obtaining the help of the
Irish Air Corps to take to the skies and reconstruct the track
taken by the ill-fated aircraft in 1968. This was done using
the witness statements of all those who contributed to the

data gathering for the original investigation, not just some of them. Therefore, using witness testimony that originated west of Waterford, a very different flight path emerged from the one that had been used as a basis for both the 1970 report and the later *Review*, and it indicated that the aircraft seemed to be trying either to return to Cork or to make an emergency landing elsewhere.

The international team's study examined the aircraft's flight path, according to the witnesses' observations, with the suggestion being made that structural degradation was occurring as the Viscount was flying. Similar incidents occurred in other Viscount accidents, but the details of these events were not available in 1968. While witness testimony now gave credence to the possibility that the Viscount was attempting to return to Cork, the study only had a brief point to make on this: that the information contained in the 'by Bannow' message was 'entirely incompatible' with the reconstructed flight path. This route showed, the study continued, 'that, at that time, the aircraft was at lower altitude, somewhere between Old Parish and the Kennedy Arboretum'. The study offered no more than this.

The team offered a possible explanation for the appearance of unusual clouds around the aircraft. The sighting of black clouds could have resulted from the engines malfunctioning, while a swirling vapour could have been fuel streaming from the aircraft. A loud noise that was reported, which was reminiscent of a motorcycle engine, might have been caused by increasing 'flutter' of the Viscount.

The newly reconstructed flight path prompted the team to enquire as to how and why the words of so many witnesses, mainly from west of Waterford, were not considered in the original investigation. On 29 August 2001, members of the team met a senior staff member of the Irish Aviation Authority. He told them that he had 'no useful comment' that would help them to solve the problem of why it was that the original reconstruction of the flight path was undertaken using, as its basis, just the radio transmissions between the Viscount and Shannon ATC, with the result that all of the witness statements from west of Waterford were rendered irrelevant. This was further confirmed to the team during the same week, when it met with someone who had been involved in the original investigation commission.

This directed the team's focus on to what happened at Shannon on the day of the crash. On 12 September 2001, its members interviewed the surviving air traffic controllers who were present on that terrible day. With a lack of any recordings to work with, these interviews were necessary, but they yielded nothing new. Of course, placing such questions before these people needed to be done in a sensitive manner, lest the line of enquiry be considered to be calling someone's professional integrity into doubt, albeit unintentionally. One former member of the ATC staff dealt with the team only through a firm of lawyers.

The team hypothesised that an initial event of some kind occurred to the tail section of the aircraft at 10.42 a.m., and that its structural integrity degraded until control was lost and the Viscount plunged into the sea about half an hour later. It veers (yet again) towards a bird-strike as being the cause, with 'new' witness statements now providing a flight path that had not been contemplated – publicly, at least – for either the 1970 report or its *Review* successor three decades later. Yet it neatly sidesteps some crucial issues. One of these is the 'by Bannow' radio message and the aircraft's actual location at that moment, while another was the floating debris observed in the Saltee Islands area.

For the third time in as many decades, very serious questions remained to be answered in the riddle of the Tuskar Rock crash. The team contacted the aerospace company BAE Systems, seeking its opinion on aspects of the study. The company's responses, on 16 August and 5 December 2001, were far from kind. The first reply was, in fact, a full seventeen-page review of the material that had been sent to the company. Some of it referred to mistakes in phrasing or grammar, which seemed unfair, as English wasn't the first language of two of the three team members. Even so, one would have thought that such material would be proofread and corrected before release. Of more importance was a comment, on the review's first page, which referred to the study as being 'not based on all the evidence, indicating a pre-judged conclusion'.

The letter of 5 December took the international team to task over how it went about the business of examining – and interpreting – the available evidence. The company 'disagreed fundamentally' on the methodology that had been applied and, by extension, the conclusions that had been reached. The scathing letter went on to criticise the team for discounting the main piece of contemporaneous and objective evidence, which suggested that the aircraft's actual location was by Bannow at 10.57:07 a.m. The company found it 'extraordinary' that the study team asserted that the ATC transcript must be 'unreliable and is to be disregarded when set against the eyewitness evidence'.

BAE Systems also pointed out that, according to the team, the aircraft had already suffered an uncontrolled dive and was breaking up at low altitude *before* it transmitted the 'by Bannow' message. The later 'spinning rapidly' communication was the first and only indication that there was any problem with the aircraft. In short, the company disagreed with what it saw as the study team's reliance on witness accounts to shed new light on what had happened thirty-three years previously. No matter what the witnesses saw, the aircraft had reported its position at Bannow and was en route to Strumble. In the opinion of BAE, the international team of experts was, in other words, trying to force square pegs into round holes to somehow come up with a solution to the mystery. Despite this strong criticism, and despite the shortcomings and the many as yet unanswered questions, the study team members still went on to state 'as a conclusion, the international team is of the opinion that the files of the EI-AOM accident should be closed'. While no crucial questions had been answered, this has been the Irish government's stance ever since.

The Tuskar Rock story has been through many twists and turns over the years, but never had such a shocking claim emerged as when, at the start of 1999, an assertion was made that the British military not only recovered bodies after the disaster, but that it systematically destroyed vital evidence of a missile strike on the aircraft, such as pieces of shrapnel, metal or chemical traces that were not part of the aircraft, by incinerating these human remains. Furthermore, it was claimed that only those bodies that displayed impact injuries were returned to the Irish authorities.

This story made the headlines in Ireland on 6 January 1999, when TV3 ran with it on its main news bulletins. By the following morning, *Irish Times* journalists Barry Roche and Tim O'Brien had penned a piece about the claim, while the *Irish Daily Star* led with reporter Fraser MacMillan revealing how the deceased were allegedly 'secretly cremated' after the crash. MacMillan and Roche presented further details in a two-page spread, but journalist Ken Foxe also detailed a denial by the British embassy. A spokesperson for the embassy stated that a planned meeting the following week between Mary O'Rourke and Veronica Sutherland, the UK ambassador, was not connected to the story in any way and was merely a courtesy visit.

The idea of the secret destruction of bodies was unpalatable to the general public, to say the least, but to the relatives of those killed in the crash the allegation must have been truly horrific. By the following Sunday, journalist John Burns revealed in a lengthy newspaper feature that the documents which led to the story were no more than a tissue of lies, produced by a private investigator who had been hired by a woman whose parents had died on the Viscount. The woman, Bonnie Gangelhoff, had engaged her lawyer to hire the private detective to look into the events surrounding the crash. The detective took on the investigation and subsequently produced documentation to Ms Gangelhoff which stated that a Sea Dart missile *had* in fact been launched by the UK military that day. The aircraft's transponder was not functioning correctly and the missile locked on and targeted the doomed airliner.

The detective was producing documents in a drip-feed manner, for which he was well paid from an insurance policy left to Bonnie Gangelhoff by her father. Her legal team became suspicious of him, with one of its members commenting that he wasn't trustworthy. There was little point in believing the detective, the team member suggested, because 'even when he was telling the truth, you didn't know'.

The investigator was permanently secretive about where he had obtained the papers he had produced. The names of his sources – if they existed at all – were known to him alone, though at one point he had said that he had a contact within the US State Department. But he couldn't be asked any more about this, Burns wrote, because he had disappeared. The story went around that he was spirited away because he was in the federal witness protection programme, though he did surface, briefly, to testify in an arson case in Connecticut, USA.

The life of the elusive detective read like a spy novel, but it was something much more ordinary that raised suspicions about the provenance of his documents: spelling and terminology mistakes, and what seemed to be the erroneous composition of the security papers he had handed over. They were stamped with a 'restricted' level classification and nothing higher. The next level would be 'confidential', then 'secret', and then a 'top secret' level of clearance would apply to those accessing the files. If the Viscount really was targeted and destroyed by a surface-to-air missile, Burns reasoned, then surely any documents that related to this terrible truth ought to have ranked much higher than a mere 'restricted' level of security classification. Also, as far as errors were concerned, there were discrepancies throughout his documents; for example, a reference to the Royal Navy's HMS *Penelope* became just HM *Penelope*.

Bonnie Gangelhoff passed the files she received on to the Irish government in 1981. The Irish authorities duly contacted the UK's Ministry of Defence, which replied that the papers had been falsified. This subsequently also became the Irish stance. Neither, apparently, ever informed Ms Gangelhoff of their verdict, and in late 1998 she passed a copy of the files on to Jerome McCormick, a representative of the relatives of those who were killed. As 1999 dawned, he sent copies to two well-known Irish investigative journalists, Charlie Bird and Vincent Browne, but nothing happened in response. Having seen the professionalism in the reporting style of TV3 news presenter Ray Kennedy – who had just covered the release, into Ireland's National Archives, of the latest batch of government documents under the thirty-year rule – he then opted to supply the (at that time) new television channel with a further copy.[1]

With the passage of time between the publication of the international team's study and the present, some further interesting information has found its way into the printed media. On 24 March 2007 – the thirty-ninth anniversary of the crash – a retired RAF officer, Eric Evers, made a startling claim while attending a meeting of relatives of those killed. At that gathering, in Cobh, County Cork, the former RAF squadron leader asserted that the Irish Air Corps had inadvertently caused the Viscount to lose control and drop from the sky. Evers suggested, a well-known Irish newspaper said, that the Irish and French governments had colluded to hide the truth.[2]

Jerome McCormick, who was present, commented to Deirdre O'Donovan of the *Irish Sunday Mirror* that he couldn't discuss what Evers had claimed, but that corroboration was slow in coming. He felt, though, that the Irish government 'may have some knowledge because, on that Sunday afternoon, there was a very important meeting held in Broady [*sic*] military airport in West Wales'. He went on to say that there were eighteen people present at the meeting in the Royal Navy's Brawdy air station, including officials from Ireland, and that the entire episode had since been denied. (The MoD stated that no such meeting was logged by RNAS Brawdy, in response to queries posed by the Celtic League and the relatives, according to the *Review of Irish and UK Files.*)

According to the former RAF officer, three red lights on the Viscount's control panel indicated to the pilot that the aircraft's undercarriage was unlocked. An option used in the defence forces to check on the problem was to ask another nearby pilot to drop down and check. Bernard O'Beirne, Evers maintained, would have been aware of any Irish military flights operating out of Baldonnel on that Sunday morning. Evers' theory was that a French-made Fouga Magister jet of the Irish Air Corps was asked by Captain O'Beirne, who had served in the forces himself, to fly underneath the Viscount and examine its undercarriage. This manoeuvre apparently resulted in the two aircraft clipping one other, causing the Viscount to lose control.

When asked about this, an Irish defence forces spokesperson told the newspaper that the idea was 'spurious' and that – as had been stated since the time of the incident – there was no evidence that any Irish military aircraft was in the area at the pertinent time.

Moreover, according to official records, the Irish Air Corps did not purchase a Fouga Magister until the mid 1970s. The French-made Fouga Magister aircraft served (and still serves) in the armed forces of many nations, though now it has largely been relegated to serving as a reserve or training aircraft, with Ireland finally replacing it in the early 2000s with the PC-9M. Based on an original concept dating from the late 1940s, it came into French service from the mid-1950s. The CM-175 version – also known as the Zephyr – was designed for deployment on board aircraft carriers, while the Irish Department of Defence finally purchased the CM-170 version in the mid-1970s.

However, this seems to be contradicted by the international team's study. In Section 5.2g of the appendix were listed and illustrated the various fixed-wing aircraft that were deployed by the Irish Air Corps in 1968. Included in this appendix were the following types: the Vickers Supermarine Seafire; Vickers Spitfire IX; the Hunting Percival P56 Provost; the Chipmunk, Dove and Vampire, all manufactured by de Havilland; and … the Fouga Magister. If the Irish Department of Defence did not obtain any of these aircraft until around halfway through the 1970s, how and why was it listed and illustrated as being in service in 1968? Deirdre O'Donovan, of the *Irish Sunday Mirror*, posed this question to the defence forces' spokesperson when she was working on the story concerning the appearance of Eric Evers at the meeting of the relatives of the victims in Cobh. The military representative would not comment to the journalist as to how the Fouga Magister could have been included in a list of Irish defence hardware in an aircraft recognition document – which belonged to the British military – generated in 1968.

The suggestion of an involvement by the French authorities in covering up the accidental destruction of a civilian aircraft – though very much unproven – was repeated by the Irish media almost six months after Eric Evers' claim concerning the Fouga Magister. The *Irish Mail on Sunday* ran a piece by journalist David Barnes, in which he reported on an interview he had conducted with a woman, Margaret Connolly, about the unexplained September 1968 death of her father, and of ninety-four others, on board a Caravelle airliner being operated by Air France. Arthur O'Connor was flying from Corsica to Nice when the aircraft crashed just 32 miles (51 km) from its destination.

The official inquiry into the disaster closed after four years, with the verdict being that the pilots had lost control of the Caravelle after a fire had broken out at the back of the aircraft. However, Margaret Connolly informed the journalist during the interview that a number of people had since come forward to express their belief that the aircraft had been struck by a ground-to-air missile being test-fired by the French military. In September 2006, an association of families bereaved by the incident had pressed for the French defence ministry to be charged with manslaughter.

The relatives based their allegations on statements given by named witnesses. One of these was Etienne Bonnet, who said that he was looking at dolphins through binoculars when his attention was drawn to an object in the sky that had a blue trail behind it. It collided with the aircraft, causing an explosion. Another person who came forward was Noel Chauvenet, who was an engineering apprentice at the time of the incident. He stated that in 1971 a technician told him that he had taken part in ground-to-air missile trials in Provence and the only one he saw working was the one that slammed into the Caravelle. Bernard Famchon, an artillery serviceman, recalled how another soldier had broken down in tears as he told him of how a training operation in which he had taken part had turned into a disaster, when a missile that was intended to hit a target made its way instead for a civilian aircraft in the area, about which not enough warning had been received by the military unit involved.

If there is any truth at all behind the suggestion that a cover-up was instigated by the French government in the case of the Caravelle, then one must ponder whether something similar might have been put into operation after the Tuskar Rock incident earlier in the same year. While there is no evidence of any of this, in more recent times the country did become mired in another controversial and deadly incident when, in 1985, members of its intelligence community were apprehended and convicted in New Zealand having blown up a ship – the *Rainbow Warrior* – belonging to the Greenpeace environmentalist group. Two people on board were killed in the attack.[3]

The appearance in the County Wexford skies of an unknown aircraft with reddish colouring is an apt description of the bright orange-red 'dayglo' paint that was applied to Irish Air Corps aircraft. However, with no Irish military aircraft logged as going missing on the date of the Tuskar Rock crash and with no British air assets being unaccounted for, an alternative possibility could have been that a military aircraft from a third country might have been involved. Interestingly, the *Review* stated that it had 'no information' that *other* nations' naval vessels or military aircraft were operating in the Irish Sea on the day of the crash. The international team attempted to research this possibility further, but its repeated written approaches to Lord Robertson, then secretary general of the North Atlantic Treaty Organisation (NATO), went unanswered.

Even if NATO wasn't involved, the possibility still exists that a Fouga Magister jet *could have been* involved, one that wasn't in Irish service. A photograph of one such aircraft was located by us on a website dedicated to historical and current military aviation. The picture showed an aircraft in a metallic finish, edged with a bright reddish colour. It looked very much like an Irish Fouga, in what looked like Irish colours, except that the photograph actually depicted a Zephyr, and not one of the Irish CM-170s. Might the witnesses have in fact seen a foreign Fouga aircraft in virtually identical livery to that used by the Irish forces at the time?

The controversy over the possible military involvement of a country other than the UK or Ireland is just one of the many that have been part and parcel of the Tuskar Rock enigma for well over forty years.

Apart from revelations in the press, still more revealing material remains in the public domain – if it is sought out. These details have seen the light of day thanks to an unflinching resolve shown by Michael O'Toole and Dermot Walsh. Maureen O'Toole oversaw the completion and publication of her husband's book, *Cleared for Disaster*, following his death, and in doing so has provided much food for thought in the Tuskar Rock story.

One of the bizarre aspects of the incident, as we have seen, was the timing of the various sightings of the Viscount as it departed on its final flight. Michael O'Toole, having just been appointed as the air correspondent for the *Irish Press* newspaper, spent three months in Rosslare during the follow-up search operation in the wake of the disaster. Some of his insights serve as a reminder of just how strange much of the story remains. For example, there is the odd testimony of a farmer – Joseph Auglim – who, at about 10.52 or 10.53 a.m. on the morning of the crash, witnessed an aircraft entering a small black cloud. He estimated the cloud as being perhaps five or six times the size of the aircraft. As it approached the cloud, he noticed a peculiar droning noise coming from its engine. The aircraft should have passed through the cloud quickly, but it instead took a 'considerable' time to do so. 'When it did emerge,' Auglim commented, 'it had dropped considerably in height and had changed course.' The aircraft was flying south, but it then suddenly turned in what were described as 'right-angled' manoeuvres and was then almost facing the direction from which it had come. The farmer said that the aircraft was 'drifting to its left' and out towards the sea.

The international team said that the appearance of 'clouds' around the Viscount could have been caused by its engines malfunctioning, fuel leaking and so on. This would hardly explain how witnesses described the aircraft being 'fired' out of the clouds. Furthermore, in the case of Joseph Auglim's sighting, the cloud was *not* connected in any way with the aircraft's engines – or to any part of the aircraft for that matter. Nor was it a spray or vapour that was following alongside. Instead, it was completely separate. The aircraft flew directly *into* it and its presence within the cloud coincided in some way with sudden and significant changes in both altitude and direction.

The flight path of the Viscount was odd, with the international team suggesting that it in fact entered two spins or spiral dives. It manoeuvred between various points and was seen all around the south-eastern corner of the country. The disturbing details include the fact that the aircraft was flying at such a low altitude that at one point its lettering EI-AOM could clearly be seen from the ground. According to Michael O'Toole, passengers could been seen crouching forward and evidently bracing themselves for impact. (Incidentally, such a low altitude may also explain the lack of radio communication with ATC.) The Viscount's altitude was so low that at Ballykelly witnesses saw it narrowly avoid colliding with a church steeple. The second (and final) dive occurred west of Wexford town, with the time of this event put at 10.58 a.m.[4]

The puzzle here is that, by this timing, the Viscount had already confirmed that it was 'by Bannow', and that it was changing its radio frequency as it entered the London FIR. How could the aircraft possibly be approaching Strumble in Wales, *and* be in difficulties over south-eastern Ireland, within a matter of perhaps a minute, if even that?

Then there is the mystery surrounding the source of an unexplained 'Mayday' being reported four times after the Viscount had already crashed. Accompanied by an automatic alarm radio distress signal, the 'Mayday' was detected at Rosslare Harbour in Ireland and at the Ilfracombe and Land's End radio stations in England. The initial belief was that the signal was emanating from a dinghy or a lifeboat, prompting a brief hope that there had been survivors from the Irish aircraft. There weren't, however, and these signals were never explained.[5]

The Royal Aircraft Establishment (RAE) missile testing facilities at Llanbedr and Aberporth in Wales, which had been eyed with suspicion following the crash, were closed on that Sunday, yet the descriptions of the reddish paintwork on the extremities of the mysterious aircraft seen over south County Wexford were reminiscent not just of Irish military livery, but also of the target drones that were deployed by these RAE facilities. In 1999 the RTÉ *Prime Time* team reported – following on from a documentary it had aired about the disaster the previous year – that the MoD had recently checked its records on the UK's anti-aircraft missile capabilities of 1968, and had found that the country had no land-based surface-to-air weapon system at the time that could have hit an aircraft close to the Irish coast. But a curious point made by the programme was that British cabinet papers relating to a missile test area in Wales were removed from the file archives in 1982, just as the media renewed their interest in the Tuskar Rock incident.[6]

The suspicion of an involvement by the British military has persisted down the years, as various pieces of debris have been found in the waters off the south County Wexford area. While the authorities have explained these items away, they have none the less shown how non-Irish military activity was being conducted in the southern part of the Irish Sea. In 1970, at Kilpatrick beach just south of Arklow, the nose wheel of a Sea Vixen aircraft was washed up. This type of aircraft usually operated from aircraft carriers, so despite the authorities' firm line about there having been no carriers operating in the area at the time of the Tuskar Rock crash, the discovery at Kilpatrick triggered further rumours. One of these was the possibility that, if the Sea Vixen had crashed during the Tuskar Rock incident and its pilot had baled out, it might have accounted for the mysterious distress signals that have never been explained. The pilot could have been picked up by any one of the dozen-plus Royal Navy vessels that had taken part in the follow-up search operations after the Viscount crash.

The MoD maintained that the debris was from a bad landing by a Sea Vixen on the aircraft carrier HMS *Hermes*, not in March 1968, but just weeks before the debris was found in 1970. As the nose wheel was made of a light alloy, it should have come ashore a lot sooner if it had actually been connected with the 1968 disaster.[7]

The passage of time between the 1983 publication of Dermot Walsh's *Tragedy at Tuskar Rock* and the Irish government's *Review* of the files and then the international team's study, has not dimmed the relevance of the book. The contrary is true, as it makes several salient points that have now faded from memory but which might still have a bearing on what actually happened on that terrible Sunday.

For a start, the original 1970 report was completed in June of that year, yet copies of it were not distributed to the country's national newspapers until two months afterwards, on the evening of 7 September, when, it might be thought, the rush to compile the following morning's competing editions ensured that no detailed press analysis of the report's contents would be carried out.[8]

One must regard pronouncements from the MoD around that time with some caution. On 11 September – just days after details of the Irish government's report made it on to the newsstands – the ministry firmly denied that there were Royal Navy or RAF exercises taking place off Ireland's east coast. Yet lifeboats had been called out from their bases at Wicklow, Howth, Dun Laoghaire and Arklow to investigate multiple sightings of what looked like distress flares. The next day, the *Irish Independent* reported that the RAF and Royal Navy were involved in manoeuvres 15 miles (24 km) off Anglesey, Wales. This exercise had managed to stray to within 12 miles (19 km) of the Irish coast and the Royal Navy not only confirmed that fact, but said that it had informed the Irish authorities about it. Yet the MoD in London denied all knowledge of what its own naval forces openly admitted.

The keeping of military secrets was (and is) nothing new, of course, but what secret military activity – if any – was taking place on the morning of 24 March 1968? When mixed messages come from a country's armed forces and its government – as in the incident mentioned above – then either a deliberate veil of secrecy or a simple breakdown in communications could very easily cause a catastrophe.[9]

The last four and a half decades have been marked by frustration at the lack of definitive answers as to what happened to the Viscount. Questions have even arisen concerning the huge cost of the salvage operation and how, in particular, the Irish government was asked by its British counterpart to carry so little of the resulting financial burden.

In a question-and-answer session in Dáil Éireann (the Irish parliament) on 29 October 1970, the then transport and power minister, Brian Lenihan, responded to a question by a member of the Fine Gael party concerning the cost of the salvage operation. The Irish authorities received a bill of something over £145,000, with just under £136,000 due to the UK Ministry of Defence.[10] Apart from the deployment of naval vessels and equipment, the work involved in searching for the wreckage of the Viscount included the use of divers on more than ninety occasions over a period of almost a month. The efforts involved were comparable to a 1959 operation in which the British military was engaged in salvaging a crashed bomber. That work cost something in the region of £2 million – a huge amount of money at that time. If the Tuskar Rock operation cost anything like that nine years later, then it is odd that the Irish government was not presented with a more substantial bill.

Brian Lenihan requested funding from Charles Haughey, the Republic's finance minister, to continue searching for debris. Lenihan sought a sum of £2,800 to compensate trawler skipper Billy Bates for his loss of earnings, as he used his vessel in the ongoing effort to locate parts of the aircraft after the crash. The money was finally released in July 1969, but the tail section – which could have been of huge importance to the crash investigation – was never found.[11]

As the fortieth anniversary of the Tuskar Rock disaster neared in the opening weeks of 2008, the case came up for discussion on RTÉ presenter Pat Kenny's *Today* radio show. On 28 February, reporter Philip Boucher-Hayes outlined the latest – and final – official version of events that led up to the disaster. This sequence of events suggests that, having left Cork Airport and routing via Youghal, the aircraft's climb was interrupted at 10,000 feet and it entered a right-handed spin. No Viscount had ever recovered from such a predicament before, but the pilots on the *St. Phelim* regained control. The aircraft then turned around Dungarvan and headed back towards Cork at an altitude of between 1,000 and 2,000 feet (305–610 metres). This manoeuvre was not communicated to ATC by radio. Then, at a point west of Ardmore, the aircraft turned back again, and headed east over Tramore Bay and then on to Brownstown Head. Yet again, this movement was not communicated to ATC.

The Viscount then turned up the estuary of the Barrow river, towards Mullinavat. For a third time, ATC received no word from the aircraft about this. There was then a sharp turn towards the east again, to the Kennedy Arboretum area, where the aircraft entered a second spin. It was only now that the '5,000 feet, spinning rapidly' message was sent. Five miles (8 km) out to sea, the aircraft lost a part, perhaps one of the horizontal tail wings. According to the RTÉ website's summary of the *Today* show's coverage of the case, expert witnesses had said that if it was the Viscount's tail that had already been seen in the water – and not another aerial vehicle of some sort, or a part of such a vehicle – then there would have been no way that the plane could have made it as far as the Tuskar Rock area before crashing.

Finally, the aircraft slammed into the waters off Tuskar Rock. The international team's study put forward the theory that the aircraft had flown for some thirty-two minutes in difficulties, yet it only reported such problems once. To cover the distance it did in that time, it would need to have flown at a high altitude cruising speed.[12]

Yet again, the by now familiar problems of bizarre timing and lack of communications arise. There is a stark absence of one crucial factor in this version of events: that the aircraft, apparently in no difficulties, radioed its 'by Bannow' message when it did. How could it possibly have flown a bizarre course to and fro across the south-eastern corner of Ireland at low altitudes – sometimes very low altitudes – and still manage to transmit a strange call at some point that it was by Bannow?

As the head of the station's Radio Investigative Unit, Philip Boucher-Hayes decided to look into how the doomed aircraft was apparently flying in different directions and at various locations, at much the same time, according to the witnesses on the ground that day. The incident produced several mysteries and the official deliberations on it had only made things more confusing. Aside from the difficult-to-answer questions concerning times, altitudes, the lack of radio communications, the aircraft's shifting location, strange clouds, an alleged attempt to persuade a witness to stay silent, a second airborne object in the area and unexplained debris and Mayday signals, there also remained the riddle of how an Irish Air Corps Fouga Magister featured on a 1968 aircraft recognition chart, the best part of a decade before the type was purchased and entered service with the Irish military.

Bringing a list of questions to Irish aviation authorities, he received no response except that no comment would be forthcoming. In this, the attitude of the aviation bodies reflected precisely the recommendation that was made by the international team in its study report on the crash – that the Tuskar Rock case file should be closed.

The mysteries surrounding the catastrophe remain unsolved. Yet the strange nature of many of the witnesses' statements have been sidestepped by successive investigations carried out on behalf of the Irish government. The appearance of something else flying in the sky that Sunday morning finally produced – in the more recent *Review of Irish and UK Files* and the international team's study – brief comments only. These sightings were incongruous with where the Viscount was at the time, yet this aircraft or device remains unidentified. Meanwhile, despite the grave political implications that the involvement of a British missile or drone in the incident would have, the later investigative works carried a considerable amount of pertinent UK military data. So a huge effort undoubtedly went into checking out this potentially sensitive avenue of investigation, but the presence of an unidentified aerial intruder around the time of the crash was put to one side.

There were other aspects to the initial inquiry that were also somewhat unsettling. In *Cleared for Disaster*, Michael O'Toole mentions that the chief investigator, R. W. O'Sullivan, believed that his telephone was bugged during the investigation. His claim could not be proved, but he believed that aspects of the ongoing investigative work were subsequently reported in the press in a distorted manner, thanks to the use (or abuse) of information gleaned from such eavesdropping.

Another problem with the initial investigation into the crash was that approval was granted for the scrapping of recovered pieces of the Viscount, before the families of those killed in the crash, or their legal representatives, had a chance to examine them properly.

If the Viscount was in fact blasted out of the sky by a missile, or caused to crash by the presence of a missile, target drone or other military aircraft, then the Tuskar Rock case would not be unique. Aside from the alleged firing of a missile in the Caravelle case, other incidents down the years have repeatedly raised suspicions of a military involvement.

Readers may be familiar with how, in 1988, the US Navy's USS *Vincennes* fired a missile which brought down an Iranian airliner. And, six years later, Swedish researchers Anders Liljegren and Clas Svahn published details of no fewer than a dozen incidents in which civilian aircraft had alarmingly close encounters with missiles or missile-like objects – unidentified aerial phenomena (UAP) – sometimes with lethal consequences.

One of these occurred on 27 June 1980, involving an Italian DC-9 jet with eighty-one people on board, which plunged into the Mediterranean while en route to Palermo from Bologna. There was no emergency radio message from Itavia Flight 870 before it crashed, killing all the passengers and crew. After bodies and parts of the wreckage were located the next day, analysis pointed towards an external explosion having occurred. Pieces of the aircraft's undercarriage were embedded in the corpses of the victims, dispelling the theory that an explosion had occurred within the cabin. Also found on the bodies were quantities of phosphorous, which is often found in missiles.

A military source contacted an Italian journalist to say that a missile had struck the plane. A decade later, at an inquest, a sergeant at a military control centre said that he had seen the plane vanish off a radar screen – even though it had previously been denied that the aircraft was being monitored. The radar echo from the DC-9 had been followed on a parallel course by a second object. A third object, on a crossing trajectory, hit the DC-9, scattering debris.[13]

An Olympic Airways aircraft, Flight OA132, came perilously close to catastrophe on 15 August 1985. Flying from Zurich to Athens, the Boeing 727 was over the border area between Switzerland and Italy when a wingless object darted past, from left to right. The missile-like device passed just a few dozen metres below the aircraft – far too close for comfort. Fortunately none of the sixty-one passengers noticed the dark brown or black projectile. Once again, no one was found culpable of this near disaster. The Swiss military had just concluded exercises in the area, during which civilian aircraft had been excluded. Military representatives said that the manoeuvres did not involve any launches of the country's Bloodhound, Rapier or Sidewinder anti-aircraft missiles. In fact, the object's trajectory indicated that it most probably originated from across the Italian border. The Italian authorities denied any responsibility for the incident, with no Italian or NATO military activity accounting for what had been seen.[14]

In their report, the Swedish researchers also cite cases in which missiles – or what appeared to be missiles – have come frighteningly close to colliding with civilian aircraft in Scandinavia. Readers who have studied the UAP subject will know that this part of Europe saw many reports of 'ghost rockets' as long ago as the years immediately after the Second World War.

On the evening of 21 April 1991, an Alitalia MD-80 jet flying into London's Heathrow Airport from Milan, had a startling encounter with an object that looked like a missile.

This occurred over the Lydd area of Kent, with the projectile passing less than 1,000 feet (305 metres) above the aircraft. The MD-80's captain, Achille Zaghetti, later made the point to Clas Svahn that he had used the term 'missile' not because he had assumed that the object *was* a missile, but because it was basically missile-shaped. It *reminded* him of a missile. Although the pilot reported the incident straight away to the air traffic control authorities, no explanation for the unknown flying object was forthcoming. While a faint radar trace had been observed 10 nautical miles behind the MD-80, no other aircraft had been in the area.

In writing about this incident, researcher Timothy Good included some points that echo something of the missile theory that evolved in the Tuskar Rock incident. Duncan Lennox, the editor of *Jane's Strategic Weapons Systems*, commented that the description of the object was more akin to a target missile or drone, rather than an actual weapon, used for air defence practice. Though the Ministry of Defence confirmed that it had ranges in both Lydd and Hythe in Kent, it stated that these areas were used for small arms practice only. Furthermore, the incident happened on a Sunday.[15] The MoD statement didn't elaborate, but it seems a fair assumption that it was implying that the ranges would have been closed on a Sunday – as the Welsh ranges were on the day of the Tuskar Rock crash just over twenty-three years earlier.

Curiously, the Civil Aviation Authority stated that it had received a number of UFO reports in which the phenomenon was described as cigar- or missile-shaped in appearance. In this, perhaps the British military establishment was admitting that certain things flying about in the UK's airspace just cannot be identified. Or perhaps it was using the UAP subject – pointedly using 'UFO' instead, to encourage a more dismissive or disengaged public or press attitude – to subtly conceal the unpalatable prospect of missile activity almost causing a major disaster in Britain's increasingly crowded skies.

Certainly, the CAA seemed to have little problem in stating that what Achille Zaghetti had observed was an unidentified flying object. The authority conducted what it said was an extensive investigation into what had happened over Kent that evening and, on 25 July 1991, it wrote to a researcher that it had closed the case, listing an Unidentified Flying Object as the cause.[16]

The 1968 disaster off the south-east coast of Ireland, if caused by missile-related activities, was not the only occasion when something unknown and of possible foreign military origin was observed making its way through the country's airspace. In May 1984, Ireland's then foreign affairs minister, Paddy Cooney, was asked in Dáil Éireann about an incident that had happened in the Tory Island area of County Donegal, in which a missile-like object was seen flying in from somewhere near the island and over the county. The episode served as a reminder that, over many years, missiles may have been launched from foreign naval vessels conducting exercises offshore and gone astray over the country, with very serious safety implications.[17] The minister commented that this Donegal 'missile' sighting would have to join 'the list of UFOs' if it couldn't be resolved. There, it might have joined the list of no fewer than eight similar sightings between 1962 and 1976 – discussed by transport minister Albert Reynolds in parliament in March 1981 – which the Irish authorities took seriously enough to commit the resources of national agencies to investigate, with no definitive results.[18]

In all the official research and investigative efforts that have been conducted into the Tuskar Rock incident over the last forty-plus years, the curious timings of the sightings of the aircraft and the unexpected directions in which it was seen travelling at these times, have never been tackled. These peculiarities and others would not go unnoticed by the investigating authorities, but they are the 'elephant in the room' that no one talks about. What if all of the witness testimony is sound? What if everyone did actually see what they *said* they saw on that day? To have an aircraft evidently appearing almost simultaneously in two places – and therefore somehow defying our accepted laws of time itself – seems like the stuff of science fiction. That said, just such instances have been reported down through the years.

If the Tuskar Rock incident did feature a bizarre displacement of the aircraft leading up to the actual time of its impact with the sea, such an occurrence has featured elsewhere in the annals of aviation. In 1993, for example, Graham Sheppard, a British Airways pilot at the time, experienced a peculiar lateral displacement while flying a Cessna 172 aircraft over Puerto Rico. On 2 March he took off from San Juan Isla Grande Airport with the intention of shooting some video footage of the Arecibo radio telescope. Having filmed for perhaps ten or fifteen minutes at and around the site of the huge telescope, his flight plan then entailed tracking towards Mayaguez Airport, on the island's west coast. His flight to the Arecibo site went as planned, as did his stint of filming there. It was then that things took a decidedly odd turn.

With his filming completed, Sheppard headed on a bearing for Mayaguez Airport, climbing up to 2,200 feet (671 metres) in altitude. All seemed well, but within a few minutes he felt uneasy and confused about his position and bearing. His heading of 270 degrees should have brought the Cessna to the coastline, at right angles to his track. However, he was shocked to find that the coastline, when he reached it, ran parallel to his aircraft instead. It transpired that he was in fact flying along the south coast of the island.

Navigational error was not a factor, as his flight control instrument readings were filmed by him during the flight away from the telescope. Any errors he had made would have become obvious when he reviewed his cockpit foot-age afterwards. There was no evidence of any such mistakes, which would have been unlikely in any case, given the vast wealth of experience he had garnered during his long and distinguished flying career. Nor was the weather a factor.[19]

At a later date, Graham Sheppard and researcher

Timothy Good returned to Puerto Rico to fly the same route, in the same aircraft. Nothing unusual happened, and the two men were left totally perplexed by the pilot's 1993 experience.[20]

This baffling spatial shift is not unheard of in that part of the world, given Puerto Rico's location in relation to the famous (or infamous) Bermuda Triangle, whose geographical area has spawned numerous tales of strange weather, the disappearances of aircraft and ships, and the presence of magnetic anomalies. The legends of the Triangle have been extensively documented elsewhere, but another part of the world in which aircraft have been affected by peculiar phenomena is the Great Lakes area, bordering Canada and the United States. It can be seen that odd episodes can and do occur in various locations around the world, and many of the witness accounts surrounding the events leading up to the Tuskar Rock air crash might not have been without validity.

The mysteries of the Tuskar tragedy remain unsolved more than four decades later. Yet for some, it would appear that keeping a lid on the case – and a watchful eye on those probing it – is the main priority. The publication of the *Review of Irish and UK Files* and the international panel's deliberations soon afterwards, attracted the attention of an avid student of Irish aviation affairs. For Paul Redmond (a pseudonym) the availability of this new material prompted a renewed interest in the incident. Redmond has studied aviation mysteries from around the world, Ireland included, and readers of our earlier book, *Conspiracy of Silence*, will be aware that he provided us with a January 1977 recording of an exchange between a pilot and Dublin ATC concerning an unidentified airborne object in the pilot's line of sight. As Redmond's interest in the Tuskar Rock case saw him conducting new research and making various enquiries, something unsettling happened.

In the late 1990s, with an increasing number of break-ins having occurred in his home area near Dublin, Redmond invested in an expensive electronic security system for his home. The system served him well for several years, until he began his new work on the Tuskar Rock case. Leaving for his job one dark winter's morning, he switched off the lights, locked the doors and windows, and set the alarm. That evening, instead of returning to a dark house, he found that all the lights in his home had been switched on. Believing that burglars were inside, his rising anger dispelled any caution or reticence on his part. He jumped out of his car and quickly opened the front door, dashing from room to room. He found no one there, and all the windows were still locked, as was the back door. The front door had not been forced open. Even so, *someone* had managed to bypass his alarm system.

The really odd aspect of this break-in was the very selective nature of the burglary. Burglary, in fact, would be a misnomer, as nothing was taken. The intrusion had all the hallmarks of having been done in a very professional manner. The house wasn't ransacked, while items such as electronic goods, ornaments, credit cards, cash and jewellery remained untouched. The only thing interfered with, apparently, was his right to privacy: his computer desk had been disturbed, with discs moved around and put back in the wrong places. His normally tidy work area had undoubtedly been rifled through and his discs checked.

Who did this and what they were looking for, either among the discs or on his computer, are questions that remain unanswered. However, there can be no doubt that those responsible wanted him to know that they had paid him a visit – hence all the lights being deliberately left on.

Despite retaining a personal interest in the Tuskar Rock incident to this day, the break-in discouraged him from pursuing the case strongly. If there is nothing about the Tuskar Rock disaster that someone wants to keep out of the public domain, then this highly unusual and intimidating break-in would seem pointless.

5

STRANGE SKIES

The Tuskar Rock disaster off Ireland's south-east coast featured the startling prospect of a doomed aircraft being observed in places where it just should not – or perhaps *could* not – have been, according to the official version of events. The experience of seasoned pilot Graham Sheppard in Puerto Rico, involving the apparent teleportation of his light aircraft from one location to another, further illustrates that the world's skies constitute a much more mysterious realm than any of us realise.

Thankfully, Sheppard's case did not end in death or injury. Unfortunately, this has not always been so. Around and across the Great Lakes area that borders the United States and Canada, aircraft have reported an astonishing number of engine and instrument failures. Many aircraft have crashed, while others have disappeared and never been seen again. Many of the characteristics in these cases were echoed in the Tuskar Rock tragedy and one might wonder if whatever peculiar phenomena manifested in these North

American incidents are closely related to those that appeared just before the demise of the Viscount in 1968.

In February 1963 a Canadian civil aircraft crashed in the Great Lakes area. On 12 February the aircraft, registration CF-LVJ, with four people on board, was observed flying towards Niagara Falls. Eyewitnesses on the ground later told investigators that the aircraft broke up in mid-air. Along with these witness statements, the investigation team also had the wreckage of the aircraft and the bodies of those who perished on board with which to conduct its inquiry and reach conclusions.

After extensive testing, it became clear that the aircraft's wing had snapped off. Yet neither stress nor fatigue caused the wing to fracture. So how could it simply have broken off, causing the fatal accident? It had been a calm day, with a surface wind of 3 miles (4.8 km) per hour. To try to explain this, meteorologists were called on to assist in the investigation. These experts sent aircraft, packed with technologically advanced equipment, through the same area to ascertain whether any atmospheric conditions could have contributed to the in-flight destruction of CF-LVJ. They were unsuccessful. Their conclusion was that some force, unknown to meteorologists and engineers, and invisible to observers on the ground, had been responsible. The force that caused the break-up had an unknown speed and strength, and it was not related to any known phenomenon.[1]

In the course of his lengthy studies of the subject of reported unknown aerial objects, conducted on behalf of the

US authorities, astronomer Dr J. Allen Hynek found that in some accounts of sightings there was a mysterious phenomenon that caused strong vibrations in the air around it. Such disturbances also affected items on the ground, even if they were quite a distance from the aerial object. An example of this occurred on 14 April 1957, when two women observed an unknown device landing about 300 feet (91 metres) away from them. The object – which was obviously a structured vehicle of some sort – was silver in colour and reminded them of a circus big top, though only about 5 feet (1.5 metres) in height. The women stated that, as the object was landing, a deafening rattle emanated from a metal road sign situated about 20 feet (6 metres) away from it. The sign was vibrating violently during the time that the object was present, with the racket still being audible from another vantage point, approximately 1,000 feet (305 metres) away.

As the object took off and moved away, it flew over a second road sign, which also proceeded to shake violently, as though it was being blasted by rapid, repeated shock waves. The UAP itself, though, remained silent. Later, when a compass was placed next to the sign, it showed a deviation of 15 degrees. Could there then be a connection between the mysterious force that tore the wing off CF-LVJ and the apparently violent forces associated with some UAP? Certainly, investigators who have recovered and examined the debris of crashed aircraft in the Great Lakes area have been dumbfounded as to the cause (or causes) of some of these incidents, as they defy logical explanation.

In his research, Hynek also received a report from a professional astronomer about an intriguing sighting in the Great Lakes area. He explained that the unidentified airborne phenomenon appeared to be controlled by some intelligence, but that he did not believe it to be a solid, physical object.[2]

On the night of 6 February 1961, hundreds of callers jammed the phone lines of government authorities looking for an explanation for the blinking objects that were being observed in the sky throughout the north-eastern United States. Neither the Smithsonian Astrophysical Observatory in Cambridge, Massachusetts, nor the North American Aerospace Defense Command (NORAD) had any explanation for what the eyewitnesses were reporting.

As this aerial spectacle played out, commercial pilot Peter Dekeith set off in a Piper PA-22 aircraft, registration N9402D. He was an experienced aviator, having flown Vickers Viscount aircraft for five years. Within minutes of taking off just before 5.20 p.m. he contacted the Joliet flight services centre, near the Chicago shore of Lake Michigan. He reported that visibility was unlimited, with just some scattered cirrus clouds present. In short, conditions for flying were very good. Suddenly the calm, professional pilot – with over 5,000 flying hours' experience – sent a disturbing radio message. In a shaky and highly agitated voice, he said that he was having trouble with his aircraft and was heading into the frozen lake. Asked to give his position, his only response was again that he was having trouble and was plunging towards the icy lake.

The following morning his aircraft was found, with the pilot's remains still at the controls. The aircraft was nose-down on the lake ice. The crash investigators found that there had been no fire and that the wreckage was, surprisingly, quite intact. The speed on impact would have been well above that for a normal landing and the engine had been developing substantial power on impact. There was no indication of either engine failure or malfunction. All the controls were capable of normal operation up to the point of impact with the ice. There was another mystery: the elevator trim tab was trimmed full nose-down, which is only selected in a high-powered rapid descent.

The cause of the accident must rank among the strangest in aviation history. All that the investigators could discern was that Dekeith trimmed the aircraft full nose-down and went screaming into the ice of Lake Michigan with the throttle wide open. The idea of suicide was discarded as it was highly unlikely for a number of reasons – not the least of which was that he was screaming out his distress call over the radio. With the aircraft's systems being operational up until impact, he could surely have averted the death dive up to the very last second. Yet he didn't – or couldn't – do so for some unknown reason, and instead begged for assistance over his radio.[3]

On Airway Victor 116, an air corridor 20 miles (32 km) to the east of Lake Michigan, a strange event occurred on 9 March 1968, when James Looker, a professional pilot with over 10,000 hours' flying experience, left Westville, New

York, piloting a de Havilland Dove with five passengers on board. His aircraft, carrying the registration N999NJ, was bound for Chicago's Meigs Airport. At 6 p.m. weather conditions were excellent, with visibility at over 12 miles (19 km).

At 7.50 p.m. Looker transmitted that he was making a true air speed of more than 190 knots, but only flying at a ground speed of 145 knots. If this was correct, then it would have meant that his aircraft was experiencing a 45–50-knot headwind. However, there was only a slight breeze at that time of the evening and because of his direction of travel, it would have to have been a tailwind. Weather balloons in the vicinity did not indicate any unusual weather conditions that might have explained his transmission.

When 20 miles (32 km) east of Benton Harbor, the air traffic controller at Chicago Center lost radar contact with Looker's aircraft. The controller advised Looker that the radar contact had been lost and the pilot responded with his altitude and position. The de Havilland's radar echo did not reappear on the controller's screen, while no response was forthcoming from the aircraft's transponder. This should have been giving a coded reply when interrogated by air traffic control, but no response was being transmitted automatically.

At 8.18 p.m. Looker reported that the weather was still good and asked for clearance to land, which was given and he was directed on to a radio beacon called 'Surf'. Yet his aircraft was still invisible to radar. Two minutes later, he reported that he had reached Surf, with his aircraft now within gliding distance of land. Clearance was given for N999NJ to fly into the control zone, but no acknowledgement came from Looker's plane. The aircraft never landed. A subsequent search of Lake Michigan discovered all but one of the bodies of those who had been on board, but there was no trace of the aircraft. The accident report described a thorough but unsuccessful effort to find it, carried out by the US Coast Guard and two private agencies, equipped with sonar and dragging apparatus.

How could N999NJ have just disappeared? Why didn't a single person in Chicago see a large aircraft crash into the lake just off shore? Why was there no distress call? What caused the crash and why were bodies found but no pieces of debris located? Some of the world's top air crash investigators have studied this case, yet no definitive answers have emerged.[4] Details of James Looker's crash investigation have long been filed away in the archives of the NTSB, with a reference to the case still appearing within official websites connected to both the NTSB and the FAA, yet the cause of the tragic events of that March night still remain elusive to these investigative bodies.

Another mysterious episode in the archives of the world's civil aviation occurred in Michigan on the evening of 6 December 1967. Pilot Lee Sanborn, aged forty-three, was preparing for an instrument landing at Grand Rapids Airport in his PA-30 aircraft, registration N8071Y. He was the only person on board and very familiar with the approach route he was on, as the airport was the PA-30's home base. Clearance was given to fly to the outer marker, approximately 5 miles (8 km) from the airport, where the aircraft was to adopt a holding pattern at an altitude of 4,000 feet (1,219 metres). This manoeuvre was to allow a United Airlines Viscount to make its approach into Grand Rapids, passing below Sanborn's aircraft.

At 6.10 p.m. N8071Y was given clearance to descend and begin its approach, but not to cross the final approach until 6.12 p.m. to ensure a safe separation of two minutes between the two aircraft. Sanborn arrived at the outer marker a little early, so the air traffic controller instructed him to make a 360-degree turn to the right. This manoeuvre would take two minutes to complete and flying this wide circle would put the PA-30 back on schedule to arrive on track for the final approach.

Two minutes later, Sanborn reported that he had completed the 360-degree turn at the outer marker and that he was now heading inbound for the final approach. He was cleared to land, and he radioed his acknowledgement. The Viscount, meanwhile, had already landed and was off the runway.

As Sanborn was on his way to land from the final approach, the controller gave clearance to another aircraft, a Cessna 402 – 'Miller 81' – to make its approach, but not to pass the outer marker until 6.15 p.m. to allow for a separation from the PA-30.

At 6.15 p.m. Miller 81 made it to the outer marker and

was subsequently given instructions to land. The travel time between the outer marker and the runway threshold was about two to three minutes, so at 6.15 p.m. the controller expected to see Sanborn's PA-30 breaking through the clouds. With no sign of the aircraft, the controller radioed Sanborn to ascertain if the pilot had a visual with the runway lights. Sanborn replied 'negative, sir' to the transmitted query, adding that he was 'just coming up on the marker now'.

Yet it had been more than three minutes since he had reported *passing over* the outer marker, inbound. The controller, no doubt puzzled, then asked Sanborn if he was coming up – instead – on the middle marker. (The middle marker is only a minor radio fix, about 0.5 miles (0.8 km) from the runway threshold.)

The pilot again answered in the negative, stating that he was now at the outer marker position, a full 5 miles (8 km) out from the airport. How was this possible? Where had N8071Y been for the previous three minutes? Sanborn had confirmed that he was at the outer marker three minutes earlier. Had he heard the controller clear Miller 81 to land? He must have known that Miller 81 was two minutes behind him. Now, the Cessna 402 was at least a minute ahead of him, yet he seemed oblivious to all of this. Sanborn's aircraft was now still just finishing the 360-degree turn that he had *already* reported completing several minutes earlier.

He sounded calm, if puzzled. 'You gave us a three-sixty back to the marker,' he radioed. The controller, in turn, was amazed. 'You said you were at the outer marker, is that correct?' he asked, alarmed. 'Negative,' came Sanborn's reply, 'we are not at the outer marker – you gave us a three-sixty back to the marker.'

It seemed, indeed, that Lee Sanborn was completely unaware of everything that had transpired in the previous four minutes. He had been given an instruction to make a 360-degree turn to the right. Now, the control tower was asking him if he could see the approach lights from 5 miles (8 km) away. The pilot was still finishing off the 360-degree turn, back to the outer marker.

A collision was imminent. Another aircraft was heading towards N8071Y, so the tower controller transmitted a new instruction to Sanborn, telling him to climb and maintain an altitude of 3,500 feet (1,067 metres), cancelling the previous approach clearance. The controller then told the aircraft above Sanborn to climb and maintain its flight level at 4,500 feet (1,372 metres). This would result in a safe clearance between the aircraft, and each of them acknowledged their new instructions from the control tower.

N8071Y reported to the controller when the height of 3,500 feet (1,067 metres) had been attained. At this time, Miller 81 stated that it could see the airport's lights, indicating that the final approach was clear. Again, the controller cleared N8071Y for the approach and he told Sanborn to report when he was crossing the outer marker. There was no response.

Dan Dietz, a twelve-year-old girl who was in her front

yard near Lowell, Michigan, was the last person to see N8071Y in flight. At 6.10 p.m. an aircraft flew over her from north to south. The aircraft was flying so low she thought that it was about to crash into her home. She could clearly see the red and green lights on the PA-30's wingtips. Terrified, the child ran into her house, locked the front door and took refuge in her bedroom. Once there, she heard a crash.

Her parents, who had been out, came home at about 6.30 p.m. After telling them what she had seen and heard, her father telephoned the Kent County Airport, then set out with neighbours to search the area. Before long, the wreckage of the aircraft and the body of Lee Sanborn were located.

In a move that clearly echoed the dismissive attitude of officialdom to certain witness testimony in the Tuskar Rock case, Dan Dietz's recollection of the time of impact was similarly ignored, even though her recall of all other details was accepted. At 6.10 p.m. Sanborn was acknowledging an instruction to descend from 4,000 feet (1,219 metres) and he should have been nowhere near the Dietz house, let alone crashing nearby. Yet, what the controllers had heard over their radio in the tower was captured on tape, with a transcript of the relevant radio exchanges being later retained by the US National Archive.[5]

As comparatively recently as March 2010, America's national aviation and transport safety and regulatory bodies merely cited 'spatial disorientation' in relation to the incident, with no comment on either the peculiar timeline of the sequence of events, or on the testimony of Dan Dietz.[6]

Again, a clear comparison can be drawn here between the reported spatial anomalies involving the flight of the aircraft at the centre of both this case and the Tuskar Rock tragedy, and the subsequent rejection of witness testimony where it does not fit into the officially acceptable versions of events.

The incident involving the PA-30 remains a mystery. The subsequent investigation found that the aircraft's clock was still functioning after the crash, as were its radios and instruments. The FAA checked all the radio navigation aids on the ground and discovered that they were operating normally.

Another puzzle was the manner in which the controls were set. The throttles were all the way back to idle on both engines, while the pilot had the landing gear and wing flap controls in the down position. Everything was set up for landing on the runway at the airport. Instead, he was for some reason 7 *miles* (11 km) away from the airport, blazing through trees in the middle of a swamp.

The controls were not set to indicate a crash landing, and in fact the autopilot was flying the aircraft. Sanborn was flying low enough to scare a twelve-year-old child, so if she could see his aircraft clearly, why didn't he see where he was? What was the problem and why was there no distress call?

THE CASE OF THE VANISHING DC-3

Peculiar events in North America's skies are by no means limited to the Great Lakes area, however, as cases discussed by aviation author Martin Caidin illustrate. His important work, *Ghosts of the Air*, carries a wealth of bizarre aviation experiences and incidents involving named pilots and air-crew.[7]

One baffling episode occurred early on the morning of 28 December 1948, in the south-eastern United States. On that date, a DC-3 with thirty-two passengers on board was standing by for landing instructions from the control tower at Miami. As it approached the airfield from about 50 miles (80 km) out, the crew could clearly see the bright lights of the city. The aircraft was at the end of a 1,000-mile (1,609-km) charter flight. The weather was good, with a light wind and some patches of cloud.

At 4.13 a.m. the pilot contacted the Miami tower. Radar locked on to the DC-3. At that hour of the morning, it was a quiet time for air traffic. A few seconds later, with the airfield dead ahead, the DC-3 disappeared. It vanished off the radar scope and into thin air, never to be seen again.

Over 200 aircraft and 48 ships searched an area of 310,000 square miles (802,896 sq. km). Nothing was found of the DC-3. To this day the disappearance remains a mystery: the aircraft simply vanished without a trace.

THE CASE OF THE LOST PILOT

Caidin also tells of a strange case which involved a well-known pilot and his equally famous aircraft. At 1.35 a.m. one morning in 1928, the experienced pilot took off from Havana, Cuba, with the intention of flying to St Louis, Missouri. His plan was to cross the Straits of Florida en route to his destination. As he began his flight, what were described as 'weird things' began to happen. First, his magnetic compass began to spin erratically. Even his EII (Earth Induction Indicator) began to point in all directions, which made no sense at all. Both instruments were going crazy and were therefore quite useless. He had no way of determining his position or heading. Looking out at the night sky, he began to use the stars for navigation, but suddenly a fog formed, making it impossible to see the sky.

As he tracked on as steadily as he could, dawn began to break. The sky, though, looked very strange to the pilot, having taken on the hue of 'dark milk' all around the aircraft. Finally, though, solid ground could be made out below, and the pilot's relief at being over land instead of the open ocean was enhanced by the fact that his compass and EII began to settle down. He then checked his position from his charts, and was completely stunned to discover that he was so far off course that it exceeded any distance he could have flown with the amount of fuel he had on board.

The aircraft involved in this weird incident was *The Spirit of St. Louis* and the pilot was Charles Lindbergh.

AN ENDURING MYSTERY

As mentioned earlier, there have been many mysterious accidents and disappearances involving aircraft (and ships) in and around the Great Lakes area, which have left investigators baffled. Charles Berlitz has been just one researcher of unidentified aerial phenomena and the paranormal to state that there have been strikingly similar events occurring in the Bermuda Triangle in the Atlantic Ocean.

It is a well-documented fact that cars in the vicinity of unknown aerial objects experience all sorts of electrical problems, which then disappear when the phenomenon departs. If such unknowns were to have similar effects on an aircraft's engine, it would obviously have catastrophic consequences for the aircraft's pilot and passengers.

Many pilots flying over the Great Lakes – Superior, Michigan, Erie, Ontario and Huron – have indeed experienced strange things before crashing. When the aircraft were recovered and examined by investigators, all electrical equipment and engines were found to have been working perfectly. Even when pilots survive the crash, they have memory loss and cannot remember their flight. We know that our brains function on chemical and electrical impulses, so the question arises as to whether the pilots' brains are vulnerable to these same strange influences that disrupt their engines and electrical systems. If so, they may act out of character and compromise the safety of their aircraft.

Whatever bizarre forces may have been at work in the

cases so far outlined, at least two other peculiar mid-air incidents have been reported by aircrew members who had taken off from the United States en route to Ireland. These incidents are described by A. A. Quigley, a retired Aer Lingus captain, in his book *Green Is My Sky*.[8] The first of these involved two very strange people on board a flight from Chicago to Dublin.

One night, probably in October 1967 – though the date isn't any more specific in the book – Quigley took off on board a Boeing 707 from Chicago to Dublin. Captain Bartley O'Connor joined him in control of the aircraft, with each man alternating with the other in flying the machine. It was a clear night with a star-filled sky as the 707 climbed up to 37,000 feet (11,278 metres) and levelled off. It wasn't long, however, before the quiet and pleasant flight took a strange turn.

The flight's senior stewardess approached the pilots, explaining to them that she and her colleagues had something of an unusual problem: the head count of the passengers had just revealed that there were now 122 passengers on board, yet the cabin crew's list at take-off had only 120 names on it. The problem was noticed, she informed the pilots, when it came to giving out the in-flight meals. The immediate quandary was resolved by taking a little food from that which had been put by for the cabin crew and making up two more meals. However, this improvisation did nothing to solve the mystery of who these two strangers were, or how they had seemingly appeared on board.

Furthermore, they had what the stewardess described as an 'unusual' appearance.

Intrigued, Quigley asked where the mysterious extra passengers were sitting. He rose from his seat, put on his cap and jacket, and made his way down the central aisle towards them. He introduced himself, and told the man and woman that he couldn't understand why they hadn't been included on the passenger list. The man replied to the puzzled Quigley, with an inflection to his voice which the pilot described as 'totally strange' to his ear. 'My name is Vaalkar,' the odd man began, 'and this is my wife. My sincere apologies to you, Captain, if you were concerned about our presence, but we joined the flight at a late stage.'

Vaalkar spoke in very precise English, with perfect pronunciation of his words. He and Quigley went on to make small talk, discussing general current events and it was a friendly exchange. Suddenly, Vaalkar's interest turned to the aircraft itself and he began to ask a series of peculiar questions, which must have stunned Quigley.

'Of what metal is this vessel composed?' Vaalkar enquired. 'Why relate your speed to that of sound? Are you limited to this method of space travel? Are you confined to jet thrust for propulsive force?'

In his book, Aidan Quigley comments that the strange man appeared to be filing away the replies to his queries as though they were being fed into a computer. While this was going on, the woman, who had been very quiet, now addressed the man as 'Sergi', and asked him to desist from asking anything further as she thought that his line of questioning might appear rude. The now completely confused pilot noted that she spoke in a 'metallic' voice.

Captain Quigley finished his discussion with Vaalkar, and made an excuse to leave. On returning to the cockpit, Bartley O'Connor poked fun at him for having been away for so long, joking that one of the strangers must have been an attractive female to have kept his colleague's attention for such a lengthy time. Quigley asked him to leave them alone for a while and to then go and see for himself what they were like.

Twenty minutes later, their 'forty [degree] west' position was passed as the 707 continued over the North Atlantic. A lot of static was being picked up on the aircraft's radio sets, with a faint whistling noise being noticed by the flight crew. Quigley mentioned (or even blamed) the aurora borealis, but the aircraft navigator informed him that something in addition to the Northern Lights must have been causing the interference. He told him that he'd been monitoring the radar scope since he'd picked up the weather ship's transmissions and there was a continuous interference trace – a phenomenon which he hadn't witnessed since the Second World War.

O'Connor, who had gone back to take a look at the two strange passengers, returned to the cockpit, puzzled. He was fascinated by their skin, which Quigley hadn't focused on because the lights were low in the cabin when he spoke to them earlier. His colleague commented on their complexion, saying that it had an 'unusual texture' and that they had the 'smoothest, whitest skin … no pores, no blemishes, no creases'.

At one point, he said, the woman dropped a magazine on the floor, and both she and 'Sergi' reached down to pick it up. So, too, did O'Connor, and it was then that he really noticed the difference between the skin on their hands and that of his own.

Apart from their skin, O'Connor also mentioned their odd clothes to Quigley. He commented that the tailoring was perfect, and that the material was strange and cut angularly. Indeed, the cut of their clothing and the way it looked on them reminded him of tailor's mannequins.

By the 'thirty west' position, the aircraft's passengers were snoozing – including, Quigley presumed, the two peculiar late arrivals. By the 'fifteen west' position, the night was drawing to an end as the 707 flew into the sunrise. Captain Quigley asked a stewardess who came into the cockpit to go back and check on the odd couple. She informed him that they were no longer in their seats and assumed that they'd gone to the washrooms.

They hadn't. They were no longer on board. Quigley made his way to row four, where they had been seated. He detected a peculiar odour in the vicinity, and noticed that the seats' headrests had flecks of a graphite-like deposit on them.

The unexplained appearance – and disappearance – of oddly behaving 'people' on board an airliner is bizarre enough, but even stranger is the reported disappearance of an aircraft over a considerable period of time. One such episode seems to have happened to Graham Sheppard's small aircraft in Puerto Rico, but A. A. Quigley mentions something similar in his book. On this occasion, nothing less than a Boeing 747, Flight 912 en route from the US to Ireland, was reputedly involved. No date is given for this event, but according to Quigley's text it occurred a few years after the incident involving Vaalkar, with Bartley O'Connor once again at the flight controls.

Canadian ATC, at Gander, was trying to call the 747. Flight 912 didn't respond verbally, but the ATC radar screen was registering the aircraft, albeit briefly. The height readout was 50,000 feet (15,240 metres), and increasing rapidly, yet the aircraft should have been at 33,000 feet (10,058 metres). Once at FL (flight level) 330, it was to follow 'track x-ray' out over the North Atlantic. Instead, it was detected on radar as being just 100 miles (161 km) off the coast and gaining altitude alarmingly. Furthermore, the radar echo was showing absolutely no lateral movement for ten minutes.

This state of affairs led the ATC personnel at Gander to think that a major fault had occurred with the aircraft's transponder. The height indicator now reached an incredible 70,000 feet (21,336 metres), yet while there was still no voice contact on any frequency, there were acknowledgements to ATC requests for a transponder identification.

The civilian ATC centre at Gander telephoned its military counterpart at Goose Bay. The indicated height of the

747 was 100,000 feet (30,480 metres), and soon the equipment was incapable of registering anything further. The military sent up an interceptor to investigate the situation, and it soon climbed to 30,000 feet (9,144 metres) to begin conducting a search around the position of the last radar echo from the 747. Parachute flares had been dropped, but no debris was spotted on the sea. At 41,000 feet (12,497 metres) there was still no sign of the 747, and with the interceptor's airframe feeling the strain, its pilot was ordered to return to base.

As the military aircraft came in to land back at Goose Bay, the 747 suddenly reappeared on radar. It was at 33,000 feet, just as it should have been, and its position was nearing 52N, 50W. Captain O'Connor's voice came on the radio at Gander, saying that he'd responded perhaps twenty times to requests for identification, asking if ATC could hear him.

Gander's response to O'Connor was that he had, in fact, been out of touch for a full hour. He checked his cockpit instruments and both altimeters read 33,000 feet (10,058 metres) while speed indications were normal. He gave an apology for making an error in his estimated time for reaching 50W, as the arrival time ought to have been 03.06 a.m. rather than 03.02 a.m., which he had told ATC. However, four minutes didn't constitute a major problem – a full missing hour did.

'You mean *04*.06 …?' Gander enquired. Yet three cockpit clocks displayed 03.00. So, too, did his own watch, as did those of his flight crew. All clocks and watches, whether mechanical or quartz crystal, showed the time as being an hour slow.

Baffled, Captain O'Connor re-set the cockpit's clocks. He couldn't understand how this could have happened, especially since they had been set to a time signal before take-off. The flight engineer checked the aircraft's fuel consumption for any abnormality: if the 747 had been airborne for an extra hour, then the rate of consumption of fuel could be detected. However, he found that there had been no such extra use of fuel.

As the flight continued, O'Connor noticed a magnificent, golden-edged cloud bank spanning the horizon in front of the aircraft. A stewardess came into the cockpit, looked at the view over his shoulder, and remarked how beautiful it was. She was sorry that the day was dawning, as it meant the end of the fantastic view they'd just had of the Milky Way.

Suddenly, as if his memory had been triggered by her comments, O'Connor recalled having a very strange experience earlier in the flight. He'd had an incredible view of the heavens, but the stars seemed to be all around his aircraft, in every direction. There were wonderful colours, explosions of cosmic matter as stars and galaxies were slowly coming into life, or fading into oblivion. He'd been aware of the passage of millennia, aeons, condensed into the time of the experience. He'd felt as if he, his crew and passengers were actually *travelling* through space. While all this was going on, he never questioned himself as to how it could be that the aircraft could possibly survive such a journey. Instead, he was enthralled by it all while it lasted, and was only jolted from this state when the ATC contacted him.

He quickly shrugged it off, but then the flight engineer informed him that he had experienced the same thing. So, too, had the stewardess who had commented on the cloud bank in front of them. All her colleagues, too, reported the same experience. They thought that perhaps some odd effect of the Northern Lights was at work. Some of the passengers also spoke of looking out at the same breathtaking view. Those who didn't witness it were asleep at the time.

Of course, it is not the intention here to state that O'Connor's aircraft and all of those on board physically travelled out into space and back again. However, their collective experience prompts the idea that they had all entered some altered state of consciousness. What could have triggered such an occurrence is a mystery, just as their disappearance off radar for an hour is a mystery, but it is interesting to note that in both of these episodes the Northern Lights – or what were presumed to be the Northern Lights – were thought by at least some of those involved to have had a bearing on events. Also, Bartley O'Connor was piloting (or co-piloting) the aircraft on both this occasion and in the 'appearing people' episode, and it was the same stewardess who had first commented to him about the strange people appearing on board and in the later flight on the fantastic view of the heavens she had just enjoyed.

Before we obtained a copy of Aidan Quigley's work, the details of these two stories had been summarised and passed on to us by two independent researchers, Paul Redmond and Greg Jarrells. Both urged caution as to the veracity of the accounts, as Quigley had gone into considerable detail on both episodes in the text of his book, but then said in his foreword that neither was true.

From studying a copy of his book, however, some facts have emerged which go against the idea of both stories having been fabricated. In his book's foreword, Quigley states that 'Bartley O'Connor' is a pseudonym, yet he also points out that he *did* know a pilot who had informed him of what he had termed 'psychic' episodes in his life, especially in his home. There, the ghostly image of an elderly woman was repeatedly observed, sometimes startling unfortunate callers to the front door.

Furthermore, the stewardess who was involved in both incidents actually told Quigley – many years after she'd left her flying job – that she also had a history of psychic abilities, which she had put down to her coming from a mixed Irish and Danish heritage.

Captain Quigley's foreword maintains that the two episodes involving the stewardess and O'Connor are fictitious, but he makes a point of writing that the 'non-mysterious' stories recounted in the very same chapter are true, with photos included to support these accounts. Indeed, the whole book constitutes a detailed look at his own career in aviation, starting with a stint flying in the Irish Air Corps during the Second World War and ending with his retirement as an Aer Lingus pilot in late 1981. A little over two years before retiring, he was involved in flying Pope John Paul II into and out of Ireland.

Overall, then, the book is a sincere work, a trip down memory lane by a retired airline pilot. Yet the mere eight-or-so pages of narrative that these two weird events merit – out of the book's total of 227 pages – are denied in no less than *thirteen* of the foreword's forty lines.

So why did he include them at all? A. A. Quigley's many and varied aviation experiences in his forty-one years of flying, and those of his friends and colleagues, are detailed in his book. These include papal flights, military service, a hijacking incident and so on. The two strange tales, meanwhile, are also inserted into the narrative, yet they merit a disproportionately long section of the foreword in an attempt to play them down.

Including them, therefore, makes no sense. Unless, of course, there is actually truth in them and publishing them in this manner was Quigley's only way of bringing them to the attention of the public without fear of ridicule. Up to the present day, many (if not most) pilots are still very reluctant to discuss any unusual aerial phenomena. One can only imagine how difficult it must have been, therefore, for someone like Quigley to speak openly about such things as long ago as 1983, when the book was completed and published.

Finally, what was possibly a hint by the author about the weird veracity of the story of Vaalkar was included at the end of the foreword. There, he writes that as a pilot friend of his was flying over Africa, he was recounting the story to his flight crew colleagues. One of them asked him to repeat Vaalkar's name. He did so, and one of their aircraft's windscreens immediately smashed.

Was this merely a coincidence? Maybe so, but a point to be made here is that his comment on this incident is made separately from the foreword's downplaying of the other two odd events. It would seem that Captain Quigley was leaving the door open as far as the reality of unusual phenomena was concerned. The basic premise of a 'psychic' pilot seeing a ghost in his own home appears not to really faze him – but transferring any sort of paranormal phenomenon from the environs of suburbia on to an aircraft does trouble him, probably for all manner of professional reasons.

Indeed, in recounting the story of the two 'people' appearing on board his aircraft, he includes his personal view that they were in fact ghosts. (But why include such a view if the account was fictitious?) The appearance of the visitors' clothes and complexion, their almost robotic tones and behaviour and their fixation with the aircraft's technology will strike a chord with readers who have studied reports down the years of witness encounters with non-human – some might say extraterrestrial – entities. This possibility, though, just might not have entered the mind-set of those who spoke with these visitors more than forty years ago.

His opinion illustrates the fact that different witnesses have different interpretations of what they are dealing with, perhaps through pre-existing personal belief systems or their cultural background, once they find themselves thrown in at the deep end as far as such disconcerting encounters are concerned. In short, what one person interprets as a ghost can be interpreted by another as an extraterrestrial, or by still another as an angel, and so on.

If they were ghosts, then they were solid enough – apparently – to not only hold and then drop a magazine, but to eat the meals that were improvised for them! It does seem odd, though, that the mind of at least one of these 'ghosts' seemed preoccupied by the capabilities of the aircraft and the materials from which it was constructed.

With Aidan Quigley's comment that his pilot friend's name was a pseudonym, the foreword also maintains – unsurprisingly – that 'Vaalkar' (or 'Sergi Vaalkar') was also not an authentic name. However, an interesting thread through the Vaalkar story was that Quigley believed not just that the odd couple were ghosts, but that they had died that very night as a Soviet space launch went awry, leaving cosmonauts to perish in a doomed polar orbit. If a husband and wife team of cosmonauts had been involved in such an awful event – presuming, of course, that their mention of them being husband and wife *was* actually true – then perhaps a lead on their identities could be established.

No such identities have been found by our researches to date. It should be borne in mind, though, that the date of the story was never definitively established in the book. Captain Quigley felt that it was most likely some time in October 1967, but could not be 100 per cent sure of that.

Also, the deaths of Soviet cosmonauts going unreported would have been nothing new in the late 1960s, according to extensive research conducted by a vastly experienced space writer, James Oberg.

In the late 1980s Oberg published some fascinating (if grisly) facts concerning the routine Cold War era cover-up of space calamities by the Soviet government. In his book, *Uncovering Soviet Disasters*, Oberg details the death of Senior Lieutenant Valentin Bondarenko.[9] He was killed in March 1961 in a fire during training for the Soviet space programme. Prior to 1986, though, no Soviet magazine or book had ever admitted he even existed.

In the early 1970s Oberg compiled a list of Soviet personnel who had reportedly died tragically while participating in their nation's efforts to gain an advantage over the United States in the space race. At the height of Cold War hysteria, he felt that something of a myth had built up in the West around such stories, but the fact remained that some personnel did 'vanish' from publications within the USSR, yet they were left in for non-USSR versions! Did such people leave the space programme, or were they drummed out? Or, one wonders, did at least some of them die in accidents?

Some of the cases listed by Oberg include the deaths of three cosmonauts in 1957, 1958 and 1959 in attempts at sub-orbital flights from Kasputin Yar rocket base on the Volga river; the death of an unnamed cosmonaut, in May 1960, when his capsule veered into space in the wrong direction; and the loss of a crew, on 14 October 1961, when their craft was knocked off course and into deep space by a solar flare.

Of course, the idea of the 'people' who appeared on board Quigley's aircraft being cosmonauts – dead ones or otherwise – can surely be discounted by the nature of their behaviour and by the bizarre questions they were asking! The only other conclusion that can be drawn is that they were *beings* from *somewhere* else.

AUTHORITIES' LACK OF RESPONSE

Questions concerning both of the incidents discussed by Quigley drew a blank when the Canadian authorities were contacted by the authors in 2008. Under Canada's Access to Information Act (ATIA), our request for information, especially concerning the incident which involved the military at Goose Bay, was turned down by the country's National Defence Headquarters in Ottawa, on the grounds that anyone making such requests must be Canadian citizens.[10]

The Goose Bay facility was operated by the US military until it was transferred into Canadian control in 1971. Therefore, queries were also put to the US aviation authorities in case that country's air traffic control apparatus had been involved in (or informed about) the unfolding events in either or both of these stories. No replies were forthcoming.[11]

The vast expanse of the North Atlantic has produced another mystery that has endured for well over half a century.

The strange demise of a US Air Force transport aircraft in March 1951 has left unanswered questions right up to the present day, with the final flight of that C-124 Globemaster remaining as a riddle in the annals of aviation history.

The Globemaster came into service just a few years after the end of the Second World War and was capable of carrying over 220 troops, or artillery pieces, or light armoured vehicles, its allowable cargo load being 50,000 lbs (22,680 kg). The aircraft answered a requirement that US forces and equipment could be transported over considerable distances at short notice, to counter the perceived Soviet threat in Europe. This threat in the immediate post-war period led to the American administration being invited, in 1948, to re-deploy units at bases in Britain that had hosted US forces during the war. The invitation was quickly accepted and acted on following the Berlin blockade of that year.

The doomed aircraft in this incident, serial number 49-244, came into service in September 1950. It had undergone a second intermediate inspection on 16 March 1951, just days before it vanished several hundred miles off the west coast of Ireland. Its final mission began at Walker Air Force Base (AFB), New Mexico, from where it flew to Barksdale Field, Louisiana, before routing to Limestone (later called Loring) AFB, Maine, USA. At Barksdale Field, Paul Cullen, a brigadier general and the deputy commander of the Second Air Force, embarked. After leaving Limestone, the aircraft's route took it via Gander and out across the Atlantic. Its destination was RAF Mildenhall in the UK, but it never arrived. None of the fifty-three passengers and crew was ever found.

At 1.06 a.m. on Friday 23 March, the Globemaster radioed oceanic control at Prestwick, UK, to say that it was making good time and that its estimated time of arrival on British soil was 6 a.m., a good half an hour earlier than had previously been anticipated.

An hour later, the next expected positional update never came from the aircraft. Its radio remained silent. Irish air traffic controllers tried to hail the Globemaster, but without success. British ATC staff alerted their counterparts in the Azores and Iceland, in case the aircraft had altered course to either of them because of mechanical problems or bad weather. This hadn't happened, though at the time of its last transmission the aircraft still had enough fuel to fly for a further eight hours or more.

The lack of any radio message was a surprise and it opened up the distinct possibility that something very sudden had happened to the aircraft. Search aircraft were scrambled, flying 1,000 miles (1,609 km) out to sea on tracks 10 miles (16 km) north and south of the Globemaster's planned route. Nothing was found by them, or by commercial air and sea traffic that had been alerted to the situation.

At 2.15 a.m. on the Saturday morning, the crew of a USAF B-29 Superfortress reported seeing debris in the water, as well as a raft – possibly upturned – and 'Mae West' life jackets 450 miles west of Ireland. However, the weather was by then very rough, and this hampered any further search for these items. By that time, no fewer than five ships and fifty aircraft were involved in the search. A USAF captain, Stanley Lankiewicz, told reporters it was the biggest air-sea rescue operation in aviation history. Hopes faded for any survivors. Poignantly, a US Coast Guard (USCG) vessel, the *Charlie*, fished an officer's valise out of the water. The USCG ship's involvement was later followed, on the Sunday, by the arrival in the area of several US Navy vessels. Two destroyers, USS *Fox* and USS *Brenner*, both of which had been en route from Norfolk, Virginia, to join the Sixth Fleet in the Mediterranean, joined the aircraft carrier USS *Coral Sea*. Three further US Navy ships joined the search: the *General C. H. Muir*, the *General Harry Taylor* and the *General Maurice Rose*. Also assisting was a Royal Navy submarine, HMS *Thule*. Before the end of Sunday, an incredible seventy aircraft were involved in the operation.

As the emergency unfolded, Shannon Airport (at that time called Rineanna) in Ireland was the co-ordination centre for the search effort. On 26 March, however, it was announced that all statements or information issued to the media would, instead, come through a US military post at Ruislip in the UK. With there being virtually no chance of anyone from the Globemaster being found alive at that time, the indications were that this decision was the start of a winding down of the effort. However, for no reason that was made public, the search was actually intensified. On the Tuesday, the *Coral Sea* launched sixty-five sorties in the search operation. The figure was thirty-six the next day

– with a further twenty-seven flying from Shannon Airport and the UK.

On 31 March, the operation was called off. The cause of the disaster was said to have been an explosion, but no reason or cause for such a blast was forthcoming. The military aircraft that had made Shannon their adoptive home returned to their bases, while naval forces resumed their scheduled duties elsewhere.

The next day, the American military announced that the search would resume and that it would continue for an indefinite period of time. No explanation for this about-turn was given. Even Colonel Oswald Lunde, the air attaché at the US embassy in Ireland, was taken by surprise at this development. In his book, *Cleared for Disaster*, Michael O'Toole delves into this story in more detail.[12] Also included is the tale of a farmer coming across some interesting debris on a beach in the Renvyle area of County Galway, Ireland, several weeks later.

On 28 April, sixty-year-old John Faherty found a small, sealed tin container that had been washed ashore. The tin, just a few inches in height and diameter, had a chipped appearance around its outer surface, as if any identifying lettering, etc., had been removed. Small flecks of rust indicated that it had been in the sea, but not for too long.

Faherty opened the tin and found a piece of paper inside with the cryptic message: 'Cullen is worried when 300 miles west of Ireland, Globemaster alters course for no apparent reason. We are going north. Have to be careful. We are under surveillance. Pieces of wreckage will be found but are not of G-master. A terrible drama is being enacted on this liner.'

The shocked farmer telephoned the garda station at Letterfrack, where Sergeant Patrick Connolly took his report. Connolly was going to Dublin on a short period of leave in the following days, and while in the city he called on the US embassy to report this development – and that the tin and its message were now in the possession of his colleagues.

Colonel Lunde duly travelled to Renvyle, accompanied by the police officer, to meet and interview John Faherty. The tin was taken to garda headquarters in Dublin for examination, with Lunde requesting that the relevant materials (and photographs of them) be passed on to him following the analysis.

In a confidential memo, Garrett Brennan, the garda deputy commissioner, pointed out that the Irish and British newspapers had reported on the loss of the aircraft extensively for a week or more in late March and Brigadier General Cullen's photo had also appeared in the public domain. Mentioning this in the memo – to the secretary of the Department of Justice – reveals caution on Brennan's part, in case the tin's message was found to have been a fake. Nevertheless, he also reported to the department's senior officer that local members of the garda had stated that John Faherty was a decent and honest individual, who would not engage in such a hoax.

No one ever did find out if the message in the tin was genuine, as both were soon passed on to Colonel Lunde – and out of the public gaze.

The lack of any definitive outcome regarding the investigation of the message found on the beach was echoed, decades later, by the lack of any relevant records being made public by the Irish government. The 1950s was a decade which saw Europe teetering on the brink of a third world war, most probably involving the use of atomic weapons. It was also a time when political sensitivities between Ireland and Britain, especially following Ireland's wartime neutrality, meant that the landing of non-Irish military aircraft in the country was something that was carefully monitored by the authorities. The minister for industry and commerce would have had responsibility in this regard, with such landings generating reams of paperwork over time.

Bearing this in mind, it is interesting to note that Michael O'Toole, while researching his chapter on the loss of the Globemaster, could locate no mention at all of permission being sought or granted for any of the dozens of foreign military aircraft using Shannon during this episode. He could find no such files in the Military Archives in Dublin, while papers from the Department of the Taoiseach that dealt with requests for military overflights and landings in 1951 didn't mention anything connected to the Globemaster search operation.[13]

Conducting the biggest-ever search operation would leave a paper trail. Or so one would think, but for some reason this incident didn't. Not in the public domain, at any rate. Maureen O'Toole finished her husband's book some time after his death in 2000, yet even a full five decades or more after the event occurred, nothing of relevance could be found by her in the National Archives in Dublin.[14]

The standard procedure for the release of Irish government departmental files into the archives follows the 'thirty-year rule'. Therefore, records concerning the Globemaster incident ought to have been released into the archives for public perusal in January 1982. Evidently, this did not happen in this case.

In 2008 Dermot Butler applied to the Department of the Taoiseach, under the Irish Freedom of Information (FOI) Act, to obtain a copy of any records pertaining to landing clearances that were given to all foreign military aircraft during the search for the missing Globemaster. A response from Patricia Williams, the department's FOI liaison officer, simply pointed out that only records generated after the enactment of the legislation – 21 April 1998 – are subject to the terms of the FOI Act. Also, she stated that particular records may be withheld for 'public interest' reasons, while records dealing with 'security' are exempt from the terms of the legislation.

Who it is that actually decides what constitutes the 'public interest' and 'security' exemptions is anyone's guess, but the fact is that the pertinent records remain out of sight and away from public scrutiny.

The story of the Globemaster's demise remains a puzzle

over sixty years later. The message found in the can on the beach only added fuel to the controversy and confusion surrounding the incident. If the note was genuine, then it prompts the possibility that something really strange was taking place on board. Most of the debris found consisted of splintered and shattered fragments, leading to speculation that a catastrophic explosion had occurred that devastated the aircraft.

The loss of the aircraft also meant the loss of many senior officers: apart from Brigadier General Paul Cullen, the aircraft was also carrying three colonels, two majors, twenty captains and four lieutenants. It was also believed that it was carrying highly sensitive documents.

Or perhaps there was another reason why such a massive operation was launched to look for the aircraft. Perhaps there was something else on board that was being sought, or maybe the efforts were to ensure that something on board didn't end up falling into the wrong hands.

The aircraft was laden with well over 46,000 pounds (20,865 kg) of cargo, and one must wonder what kinds of equipment could have been among that huge weight. Officers of the Strategic Air Command (SAC) were on board and it was a role of the SAC to keep aircraft carrying atomic bombs in the air around the clock. Globemaster aircraft were used for carrying such weapons.

Of course, it wasn't to be expected that America's military would, even after all these years, confirm that an atomic bomb *was* on board. Even so, over 190 pages of data on the incident, obtained by Dermot Butler in 2008, provided details that were not widely known in Ireland or elsewhere beforehand.

US MILITARY DATA

When conducting research into military matters, patience is often required – and this case was no exception. Initial queries sent to the Pentagon in mid-March 2008 resulted, three months later, in the USAF's accident report being located in the archives of its Historical Research Agency (HRA) at Maxwell AFB, Alabama.

The HRA file details how an *Irish Times* journalist, Arthur Quinlan, had caused some annoyance to the USAF at the time when the search operation had been quietly slipping out of the front page headlines. On 4 April 1951, a Reuters news agency report from Shannon mentioned that a senior USAF officer had stated that the retrieved debris from the Globemaster had indicated sabotage.

It is evident from reading the correspondence between various offices of the USAF that this claim caused consternation. The Air Force Office of Special Investigations (AFOSI) became involved, with AFOSI personnel – Lieutenant Colonel D. G. North and Special Agent Donald Jaynes – joining Colonel Lunde in trying to discover where the Reuters account came from. However, neither Reuters nor the London Press Association would reveal the name of their source.

The investigation concluded when Quinlan admitted

that he had in fact written the original story, though he refused to say who had – allegedly – mentioned the indications of sabotage to him. His account, which had appeared in *The Irish Times* on 3 April, came at a time when there were no longer USAF officers or personnel based at Shannon – let alone any US military publicity or media staff who might have been in a position to confirm to him that sabotage was being seriously considered as a cause of the disaster. Furthermore, the AFOSI material states that Colonel Lunde had confidential discussions with members of the staff at Shannon, many of whom disliked Quinlan for the methods he employed to make a dramatic headline.

Colonel Lunde and the AFOSI officers had provided a solution to the reports of sabotage that had originated in the Irish media and been taken up by the press in London. It is curious, though, that the AFOSI only opened its investigation on 6 July, well over three months after the demise of the aircraft and the appearance of Quinlan's claim in the British press.

Colonel Lunde's investigative efforts in Ireland played down the 'sabotage' theory – and dispelled the idea that someone had leaked it to a reporter, but the AFOSI's interest in pursuing it in the first place ties in with the fact that, behind the scenes, the prospect of sabotage did, in fact, arise. The HRA file, which includes images of small pieces of debris being kept under guard, goes into some detail on this point. An analysis of the splintered debris at the Directorate of Flight Safety Research at Norton AFB indicated that the 'separation of the pieces of flooring from the C-124 was due to an upward force from under the floor'.

The spectrographic laboratory of the Douglas Aircraft Company examined sixty-two items of wreckage. It could not determine the cause of the aircraft's loss, but there were indications that the Globemaster was on fire while still airborne – and that an explosion had occurred at some stage, though whether this had occurred in mid-air or in the sea remained undetermined.

The Douglas laboratory also indicated that 'a fragment of a magnesium coating was found stuck fast in the outside surface of a recovered section of tank crate. It was determined that this fragment came from a tubular-like section of an estimated two-inch diameter. This fragment has not been identified as having been any part of the airplane or its cargo.'

The documentation points out that the AN-M-50, a four-pound incendiary bomb that was used during the Second World War, contained aluminium, manganese, zinc, and other impurities such as copper, lead, iron, silicon ... and magnesium. Could such a device have either been carried on board and detonated, or planted at one of the aircraft's stops? Among the many pages bearing a 'restricted' classification in the report, there are details of the investigations that were later undertaken to ascertain that the aircraft had been properly secured each time it had landed before heading for Europe. At all times, it had been watched – except at Limestone AFB, where it was left unguarded for a short period.

In the search operation, one aircraft crew reported glimpsing what looked like parachutes floating on the surface of the sea. Had they simply been among the thousands of pounds of cargo that ended up in the water, or might someone have attempted to jump from the aircraft? This must be considered, as an FBI report in the file, which it submitted on 1 February 1952, said that its analysis and comparison work on the handwriting on the note found in the can on the beach yielded no 'definite conclusions' about its source. Someone on board *could* have written it.

Although many of the documents in the report carry a quite standard 'restricted' stamp, a fascinating page is also reproduced which bears an 'incoming classified message' heading. Sent from the USAF's Commcenter at its headquarters in Washington to the deputy inspector general at Norton AFB's Flight Safety Research Branch, it indicates that the members of a ship's crew in the area of the Globemaster's destruction reported what they initially thought was a parachute flare in the night sky. However, as they watched, the 'flare' separated into what the incoming message calls 'three stars'. The Commcenter asks to be informed if anyone else reports 'unusual' sightings in the area. The report does not include any response from the Flight Safety Research office giving details to Washington of any further odd sighting reports in relation to the Globemaster incident, but neither is any explanation offered.

The cases that have been outlined here are reminders that unusual events can and do occur in the skies above us.

The 'flare' incident just mentioned, which wasn't officially explained, serves also as a reminder of another aspect of aerial mysteries which continues to intrigue in the second decade of the new century. It is the realm of unexplained but very solid and very real airborne *objects*, and of reported contacts with otherworldly intelligences.

6

SCIENCE, THEORY AND UAP

There can be no disputing the fact that unidentified aerial phenomena exist. While the vast majority of reported unknown airborne objects can be explained in rational terms, a small percentage cannot. Are such 'true' cases therefore of extraterrestrial (ET) origin? One astronomer has had the courage to pin his colours to the mast by saying that the ET hypothesis does have merit and that, in at least some cases, the prospect of extraterrestrial visitation to our planet deserves serious consideration – and scientific scrutiny. His story is a fascinating one and it has led not only to ground-breaking research, but also to an increasing level of serious interest shown in the subject of UAP by a number of those in the world of science.

In July 2005 NASA successfully carried out a mission, named 'Deep Impact', which landed a probe on the Tempel 1 comet. What wasn't widely known at the time was that the mission was being contributed to by an astronomer in a privately operated observatory near Boyle, County

Roscommon, in the north-west of Ireland. Images of the comet were being captured on every clear night by using one of the observatory's telescopes, as part of an international monitoring team. The observatory was Kingsland and the astronomer was Éamonn Ansbro.[1] As an independent and outspoken astronomer – the exception rather than the rule in conservative science – he had also turned his hand to an area of astronomy that was frowned upon by many: the search for signs of the elusive 'Planet X' in our own solar system.

Journalist Antoinette Fennell compared his steadfast determination to that of William Parsons, the Third Earl of Rosse, who, in the mid-1800s, built one of the world's largest telescopes on his lands at Birr Castle in County Offaly. Parsons sought to prove that galaxies other than our own existed and that they could be observed. He succeeded in doing so. Well over a century later, Éamonn Ansbro constructed all the equipment he required to study the sky. One piece of equipment, a one-metre robotic telescope which he had designed and built, was reported by Fennell as the largest operational telescope in Britain and Ireland.[2]

Ansbro's determination to familiarise himself with astronomy was evident from a young age when, at the age of sixteen, he took an O-level in the subject using Patrick Moore's *Teach Yourself Astronomy* book as his guide.[3] By that time, he was already a member of the Brighton Astronomical Society and the British Astronomical Association, and through their meetings he had met several famous names in the world of astronomy. As time passed, his thirst for knowledge was joined by a gift for invention; he constructed a furnace to smelt metal pistons from old cars to produce telescope mountings. This led to his establishment of several companies down through the years, producing optical fittings for all manner of items, from pollution monitoring installations to street lamps and television projectors. (More recently, and following several years of development and testing, 2011 saw his commercial launch of a lens fitting for television screens that created a 3-dimensional effect.)[4]

Éamonn Ansbro discovered a star – actually a nova, *Vulpecula* – in 1976. However, his work in astronomy has also had other highlights. In 1974, for example, he was the co-discoverer of a hydrogen envelope around Saturn's rings and in 1975 he detected moonquakes, which were later verified by NASA.[5] In another aspect of his work he pulls no punches. His keen interest in the subject of unidentified aerial phenomena, his involvement in the Search for Extra-Terrestrial Intelligence (SETI) and his dedicated research into the Search for Extra-Terrestrial Visitation (SETV) projects, have raised the eyebrows of many of his peers. His fascination with this area has led to some interesting events, but it all began with many unusual sightings by members of the public in the south-west of Ireland, after he had moved there at the start of the 1990s.

He was given the names and addresses of individuals living in the region who had contacted the National Planetarium at Schull, County Cork, to report that they had seen unusual objects in the sky. After his initial conversations with these witnesses, he was confused by what he had heard, as he could not fit these reported phenomena into any category that he knew in astronomy – or meteorology, in which he had trained and worked as a young man in southern England. There was a consistency in the reports, some of which were sightings by individuals and some by several people simultaneously. The witnesses impressed him: they were a cross-section of local society, from farmers to factory workers and respected business owners. With few exceptions, they seemed to be reliable, stable and sound individuals.

After these preliminary meetings, the cautious astronomer began to read up on the subject. He ordered specialised books from stockists in Dublin and the United States, and in late 1991, he wrote to a number of organisations around the world in his search for further information, as well as obtaining the most comprehensive computerised data possible about sightings, including reports dating back to the 1940s.

In April 1992 he presented a workshop on the subject at the Schull Planetarium and met more people who had observed unusual airborne objects. Their experiences were consistent with the reports that he had already received. His reading revealed that the cases he was now researching had many features in common with thousands of others around the world. He decided that whatever was going on – and in the Bantry Bay area of County Cork in particular – merited a serious scientific approach. Because he was not restricted by being a member of any particular organisation or government body, he had a free run in following this up. He decided to hold additional workshops in various locations to ascertain whether there were other people who had had first-hand sightings in the south-west of Ireland. Twenty such gatherings were held in other locations around West Cork and in County Kerry.

At the workshops, it always surprised him to see the large numbers that attended, with some people travelling up to 70 miles (113 km) to be there. Not only were there many people who were interested generally in the subject, but there were also a significant number of individuals who had themselves witnessed strange phenomena in the sky. Some of their accounts were quite dramatic. For many of these people, it was the first time they had had the opportunity to talk with others who had undergone similar experiences: most had remained silent because of fear of ridicule, or they had deep concerns about what their neighbours might say or think.

After these workshops, Ansbro was often invited to the homes of individuals whose experiences merited a fuller investigation. Most weeks, he drove some 20–30 miles (32–48 km), bringing recording equipment, questionnaires and sometimes a video camera. He was careful to make sure that he just listened to the individuals, to avoid influencing people's descriptions of what they had seen or experienced. Being independent in this research was a good thing, as he didn't want to be influenced by the philosophy of any of the myriad research groups in existence, though he had by now read materials from many of them. He was familiar with the investigative procedures and codes of practice applied by such bodies as the British UFO Research Association (BUFORA), and these proved helpful. After completing each report, he filed all the data on a computer and plotted the locations of the various incidents on a map.

Over 120 investigations were carried out, including thirty-five that were particularly extensive (some details on cases in the Bantry area were published in our book, *Conspiracy of Silence*).[6] The results were compared with the computerised data about the thousands of reports from the US, the UK and other locations around the world. His work showed that what was happening in Ireland in relation to the sightings was consistent with what was occurring in other countries around the globe. It seemed that cultural influences did not distort the descriptions of the sightings, whether they took place in Africa, Asia, mainland Europe, the Americas, or within Britain and Ireland.

By then he had heard reports from witnesses about sightings in Ireland that dated back to the late 1960s. Such incidents were only then being spoken about for the first time. Some witnesses told him they were only willing to talk as long as they could remain anonymous. They didn't want any intrusion from the media and very definitely didn't want to risk exposing themselves or their families or friends to local finger-pointing and ridicule. The people with whom he dealt, however, may have been anything but the first (or only) individuals to have seen unexplained phenomena in the skies, though they might have felt that way. In fact, there has been speculation and research revealing that non-terrestrial visitors may have been present on or around our planet for many thousands of years. There have been similarities in such accounts recorded by the ancient Sumerians and Egyptians. Robert Temple, a Fellow of the Royal Astronomical Society, is one scholar who has spent decades researching possible contacts between extraterrestrials and humans in ancient times. Zechariah Sitchin was another who studied this area tirelessly, right up to his death in late 2010.

In May 1992 Éamonn Ansbro received his first report of what seemed to be a physical encounter with the occupant(s) of one of the airborne objects observed in the West Cork region. Unusually, the witness had initiated the contact himself, by mentally inviting the unknown *craft* – which is what it appeared to be – to come closer. He watched it approaching … and then became consciously aware, apparently a moment later, only to realise that a full *hour* had passed. By then, the craft was gone. This 'missing time' phenomenon is a recurring aspect of close encounters and readers will recall how something similar was also reported on a passenger aircraft in one of the bizarre Aer Lingus episodes recounted in Chapter 5. The individual involved in this case happened to be a close and trusted friend of Ansbro, yet Ansbro didn't know how to interpret his experience, especially as there were no other witnesses to corroborate what had happened. The only certainty in the astronomer's mind was that *something* had indeed happened, because whatever it was had put his friend in hospital for a number of days as a result of emotional trauma.

In September 1993 another witness got in touch with a similar story to tell, but on this occasion there were several other people at various locations who all saw the anomalous object at the relevant time. These two cases, but particularly the latter one, represented a turning point for the astronomer. While he had always tried to stay at a professional arm's length in his research work, four hours of filming and interviewing the witness about the September 1993 encounter had left him drained and shaken. When he had left the witness's home and got into his car, he caught sight of himself in the rear-view mirror and was taken aback to see how pale he was. It turned out that this episode had taken place only a mile away from his good friend's close encounter in May 1992.

It is not uncommon that some individuals experience difficulty in integrating such profound encounters into their lives. In May 1994 Ansbro had a lengthy discussion with Dr John Mack, a Harvard Medical School professor of psychiatry, who specialised in research on people who reported physical encounters with entities, apparently within an environment which the witnesses had taken to be inside an unknown craft. Mack told Ansbro that the September 1993 incident was one of the most extraordinary and convincing cases he had ever come across. It was one of the first cases to come to his attention where there had been independent sightings of the object at the actual time of an individual's encounter experience.

In a fascinating case study, the principal witness of the September 1993 incident had mentally invited the object – which was *very clearly* a craft of some kind – to come closer. On previous occasions, while alone, he had seen distant, brightly lit objects in the sky. Now, independent eyewitnesses supported him. Until this happened, sceptics could (and did) suggest that the likes of aircraft, satellites, flares or meteors were all that he was observing. In other words, the 'usual suspects' in so many reported sightings were wheeled out, again and again, to try to explain away everything that he had reported.

However, on the occasion when he mentally requested the craft to approach, he was in the company of his father. Both men later recounted seeing a massive object looming over them. They described it as being about the size of an aircraft carrier. The scene was reminiscent of politician Jimmy Peppard's sighting in Trim, County Meath, in 2008 (see Chapter 2) and the sheer size of the object was akin to one which many witnesses had observed over Phoenix, Arizona, in March 1997.

The concept of telepathic communication with whomever/whatever was flying this object was an interesting one and it led to further study in this field being undertaken by Éamonn Ansbro. Certainly, such a pursuit went against the grain as far as the broader scientific community was concerned … but then again, as already stated, he was free of the worries that routinely befall many of his peers, such as what others in the profession might think or, perhaps of more relevance, where the next grant cheque would come from if one's area of interest, study or experimentation rocked a very conservative boat. Besides, if the Central Intelligence Agency (CIA) saw enough potential value in 'remote viewing' to throw dollar after dollar into studies of it during the Cold War, then why shouldn't it be studied now?

The mid-1990s saw him establishing links with various biophysics researchers and, having studied the work in this area undertaken by investigators such as Rupert Sheldrake, he reached the conclusion that everything, animate or inanimate, is connected in a subtle but very real way. Sheldrake had conducted numerous experiments which documented this communication between organisms across distances in time and space. He called his theory 'morphic resonance'.

In 1995, having come across an article about the research work of aeronautical engineer T. Roy Dutton, in a BUFORA publication, Ansbro applied the results of his own extensive investigative work to Dutton's astronautical theory – and came to a very interesting conclusion. Dutton had a computerised database of 1,300 good-quality sightings from around the world, dating back to the 1880s, and he finally developed a model that matched the data. He could calculate the orbital tracks of the anomalous objects and he was confident that their appearances could be predicted.

That July T. Roy Dutton and Éamonn Ansbro began to correspond with one another, and it was discovered that no less than 80 per cent of the Cork and Kerry region's sightings, logged by Ansbro, matched the most likely times for appearances suggested by Dutton's time graphs for the Bantry area. The application of Dutton's research, in conjunction with his own findings, led to Ansbro's involvement with the Irish Centre for UFO Studies (ICUFOS) in attempts to induce appearances at various locations around Ireland as the 1990s passed. Some of those present saw anomalous phenomena in the sky and some didn't … but unusual things *were* caught on camera. On one occasion at Bantry, members of a British television camera crew who were filming the ICUFOS group at work, were left badly shaken when an unknown aerial object duly appeared.

Going public with predicted sightings seemed to be putting one's head on the block, professionally speaking. Again, though, credit is due to the astronomer for daring to tackle this problem in a new way, while many others in science had (and still have) instead chosen to simply ignore the issue, perhaps in the hope that it will eventually just go away. Ansbro wasn't merely exploring the nebulous world of the power of the mind, though. Rather, he was determined to shift the study of unexplained phenomena in our skies into the arena of serious scientific examination by using some lateral thinking. The concept of telepathy and remote viewing was certainly 'thinking outside the box' for a scientist – which he knew all too well – but his intention was to then use instrumentation to record and analyse whatever might appear. This was, after all, what science was supposed to be about.

If such phenomena – that is, the small percentage of 'true' UAP that could not be explained away as misunderstood natural events or conventional aircraft – were coming to our planet from somewhere out there in the cosmos, a theory was needed to suggest which routes such intelligently piloted (or controlled) craft were using to get here. Drawing on his experience and knowledge of astronomy, Ansbro provided just such a theory in a series of six features he had published in 1992 and 1993 in *Astronomy & Space* magazine, the journal of the Astronomy Ireland organisation. The final two articles, 'Alien Corridors' and 'Model for UFO Predictions', set out his idea that such objects – whether inhabited vehicles or automated probes – would approach Earth from certain star-, planet- or lunar-related orientations. He arrived at his hypothesis having used as a cut-off point that such visitors might originate from among the 300 stars within sixty light years of us, and he allowed for the fact that, needless to say, some non-orthodox propulsion systems would most probably be involved.

In the months, and then years, following his involvement in the 120 case studies he had carried out locally in the County Cork area, his research material was re-read and re-studied. Despite the passage of time, the witnesses never once wavered in their accounts of what they had experienced or seen.

In the search for a location with less light pollution, the late 1990s saw Éamonn Ansbro's arrival in Boyle, County Roscommon, and his first steps in the design and construction of the telescopes at Kingsland Observatory.

The 1990s had begun with him being asked by Hermann Van Belligen, an astrophysicist who was the director of Schull Planetarium, County Cork, to look into the many strange sighting reports the facility had received from throughout the Irish south-west. By 1993–94, fascinated but perplexed by what was being reported locally, he was coming across unusual results that he couldn't understand when using a magnetometer, gravitometer and Geiger counter at places where sightings had taken place.

In 1997 several predictions of appearances were made to the media by Ansbro, who had by now been joined and assisted on-site by other researchers, such as Alan Sewell and his ICUFOS colleagues, and Betty Meyler of the Western UFO Society (later the UFO Society of Ireland – UFOSI). Those involved in both groups, and Ansbro himself, were all too aware of how negatively a sceptical press (and public) might react, but it is worth repeating that eighty per cent of those sightings reported in the County Cork area corresponded with the likely times for such appearances suggested by the work of T. Roy Dutton.

The media lapped it up, especially during the summer, when column inches are routinely filled with 'silly season' fare, yet the fact remains that the press *did* attend and did see (and record) unidentified objects overhead for themselves.

On 21 April that year, thirty local people who attended an arranged sky watch at Coomhola, Bantry, County Cork, saw a group of three airborne anomalies at a distance of about 3 miles. If they were conventional aircraft, or satellites, then they surely would not have remained stationary in the sky for well over twenty minutes, and if they were stars then one of them certainly would not have broken away from the formation to approach the gathering and duly terrify the aforementioned UK television camera crew. Needless to say, perhaps, only a few seconds of footage from this entire incident was ultimately broadcast on 26 June 1997 in a resulting documentary, *We Are Not Alone*, made by Carlton Television for Britain's ITV (Independent Television) network.

On that same day, another gathering of about 400 members of the public attended an advertised event. Two aerial objects appeared, they were watched for about five minutes and videotaped by RTÉ, the main Irish television station.

On 14 December that year, in the Lough Key Forest Park near Boyle, County Roscommon, about twenty-five people witnessed a brightly lit UAP from various vantage points, and it was captured on video. On 28 February 1998 the images were broadcast on RTÉ's *Late Late Show*. The programme's presenter, Gay Byrne, insisted that the anomalous bright object on screen 'could have been a street lamp' or similar. Both of us have repeatedly visited the spot from where the footage was shot: there are no street lamps, or any artificial light sources, at the location. There are only acres of forest. Also, what wasn't mentioned on air was that at the very moment when this bright object appeared, magneto-meters at one of the nearby observation points suddenly indicated strong reactions to *something* in the close vicinity.

What was an eventful decade ended with the Ansbro household moving north to live near Boyle. It was the end of an exciting, educational period, but the new millennium brought with it new opportunities to explore this remark-able aspect of astronomy.

The first decade of the new century saw Ansbro – along with his wife, Catherine Overhauser – concentrating more on the business aspects of their pursuits, with the ongoing design, manufacture and marketing of high-tech optical equipment. Despite the need to earn a living, however, there was still time to conduct continuing research in various areas of astronomy.

By mid-2006, for example, the Kingsland facility was well established and its primary focus was on studying Edgeworth Kuiper Belt Objects (EKBOs). Writing a tech-nical, five-page feature in *Astronomy & Space* magazine at that time, contributor Mike Foylan outlined how the obser-vatory's two main telescopes, a 36-inch and a 16-inch, had by then been fully automated and programmed to capture a mosaic of images of the sky. These pictures could then be analysed when time permitted. The study of EKBOs was being undertaken in conjunction with research astronomer Apostolis Christou, who was in Armagh Observatory in Northern Ireland.

Furthermore – and given Ireland's unpredictable weather

– the prospect of cloud or rain did not prevent studies of the sky from taking place. This was because, since 2003, Kingsland had also been involving itself in radio astronomy. A window of frequencies from 5 MHz to just over 300 GHz was available to the radio astronomer and Ansbro had designed and built a 3-metre dish to study a range of suitable frequencies.[7]

The feature also told of a camera platform that had been constructed at the observatory. The unit consisted of ten mounted cameras which, between them, could view the entire sky from horizon to horizon. The mounting formed part of a tracking system which could detect – and follow – fireballs and meteors as they entered the atmosphere, and could record images in the infrared range. The 'Kingsland Imaging System' could analyse the spectrum of an airborne object moving across the field of view. The goal was to achieve a better understanding of the methods of propulsion any unknown aerial objects might be using, if any of them were not naturally occurring phenomena.

The system successfully detected many moving items as time went on and many of these were meteors. Many of the objects that travelled more slowly across the sky were found, after analysis, to be conventional aircraft. Satellites or the International Space Station (ISS) were also repeat visitors to the hunt for anomalies. In figures released to the authors on 22 March 2011, the all-sky camera system had, by that time, detected the following: 5,315 aircraft (most of them at high altitude, with others in descent to Knock Airport, County Mayo); 152 helicopters; 282 passes of the ISS; 328

Iridium satellites; 4,162 passes of other satellites; and 3,182 meteors. Twenty-six fireballs also featured in the statistics.

Some anomalies did accrue over the years, however. Four 'darting objects' were detected, as were twenty-three 'unknown' objects. Also, the Kingsland Observatory figures included no fewer than five incidents of fast-moving, cigar-like airborne objects being detected. Four 'bright, circular constructs' were also picked up and, on two occasions, what were described as 'multiple objects' in the sky were captured by the imaging system. Indeed, on five occasions, unidentified groups of objects were 'squaring' into formations in the sky. How could such incidents *possibly* occur naturally?

Éamonn Ansbro stated that the unknown objects were simply too bright for any structural detail to be clearly discerned, but the fact remains that subsequent analysis of the data revealed that the timing of no fewer than eighty per cent of these incidents – again – correlated with the Astronautical Theory.

The efforts being made at Kingsland were receiving the attention of the broader scientific community, thanks in no small part to Ansbro's submission of a paper at the Third International Conference on Optical SETI at San José, California, in the last week of January 2001. The gathering, run under the auspices of the Society of Photo-optical Instrumentation Engineers (SPIE), was given an outline of Dutton's Astronautical Theory and told of the importance of deploying state-of-the-art optical monitoring equipment. In developing and deploying his Kingsland Imaging

System, he had in fact responded to a suggestion from Scot L. Stride, an engineer at NASA's Jet Propulsion Laboratory, that ground-based robotic monitoring stations should be established to gather technical data from a range of sensors in a search for any hypothetical interstellar robotic probes, especially between Earth and the Moon.[8]

Such anomalous phenomena might not necessarily be at a very high altitude or even outside the atmosphere, as events in Bantry (and all around the world) had shown. Indeed, events in Norway in the mid-1980s had demonstrated just how close such encounters could be. A scientific team, directed by Erling Strand, associate professor of engineering at Ostfold College of Engineering near the Hessdalen Valley, was established at that time to undertake research into unusual aerial phenomena that had been observed in the valley area. The phenomena that had been seen were multiform in their appearance, with reported sightings dating as far back as the 1890s. Were they some form of naturally occurring event, such as marsh gas or even ball lightning, perhaps? In an attempt to find out more, the research team undertook an intensive, on-site monitoring operation that lasted for thirty-five days in January/February 1984. The team comprised a multi-disciplinary range of specialists in atmospheric physics, geophysics and engineering.[9]

The group's five weeks of observation yielded some very curious results. Having deployed telephoto lenses, an infrared viewer, a seismograph, radar, a Geiger counter, a magnetometer, a radio spectrum analyser and laser equipment, Strand

and his colleagues had recorded a wealth of puzzling data. Though the optical equipment was relatively unsophisticated by today's standards and was thus inadequate to obtain highly detailed close-up visual data, the team members were still very successful in obtaining significant results from their radar, magnetometer and radio spectrum analyser.

To begin with, the luminous aerial phenomena that were observed had a very marked radio signature, and were seen to have a fairly regular pulsation. This pulsation rate altered immediately when a laser was pointed at the anomalies. Also, the research team recorded sudden oscillating radio spikes of unexplained origin. These radio spikes did not usually occur when the luminous phenomena were present. However, in conjunction with the appearance of these bright objects, the monitoring team detected pulse-like magnetic readings.

Whatever was causing these peculiar events appeared to be repeating itself elsewhere, as the same research team detected strange magnetic pulses – and saw similar luminous phenomena – in the Australian desert and at a major volcano in Mexico. In both of these cases, inexplicably, the magnetic pulses were of a factor ten to a hundred times higher than those measured at Hessdalen.[10]

This pattern of seemingly related luminous and magnetic phenomena could have a significant connection with the reported magnetic interference on electrical devices, apparently caused by the close proximity of reported *structured* UAP. (In other words, possible craft of unknown origin.)

One such incident was reported by researcher Joseph Trainor in 2002. On 1 July that year, five police officers in Argentina, in two patrol cars, observed what a local newspaper described as 'a strange luminosity' over their heads. The 'powerful light' manoeuvred around the night sky and then approached the two squad cars, which were parked at a truck stop at the crossroads of Routes 6 and 39 in the country's Parana district. The startled officers reached for their side arms but the object, seemingly unfazed, continued to fly about the area for a further half an hour before departing the scene.

During this incident, the cars' headlights lost power, and the vehicles' ignition systems would not function until after the phenomenon had gone.[11]

CAREFUL CONSIDERATIONS

Erling Strand was among the first scientists to stress that a great deal of deliberation is required to ensure that those seeking evidence of possible extraterrestrial probes are not misled. To this end, further research is needed in places such as Hessdalen, in case natural phenomena – albeit previously little understood or completely unknown ones – lie behind the visual, radio and magnetic effects recorded.

Éamonn Ansbro's San José paper made the point that even if unusual natural phenomena were present at Hessdalen, such as tectonic stresses and the piezoelectric effect, for example, there might have been an overlapping of natural *and* technological occurrences there.

Strand's efforts are praiseworthy. As with many scientific studies, though, funding was always going to be a stumbling block, and a more low-key scientific presence was established at the site, culminating in the Hessdalen Interactive Observatory becoming operational in 1998.

Though largely forgotten by today's scientific community, two earlier attempts had been made to use monitoring stations to observe, study and measure anomalous aerial activity in the atmosphere. In Austin, Texas, Ray Stanford established a fixed monitoring station for three years in the mid-1970s. The findings of Project Starlight International were that the events being studied did indeed have an infrared component.

The 1970s also saw physicist Harley D. Rutledge leading Project Identification. Based in Missouri, he and his colleagues were able to calculate the distance, velocity and apparent size of unknown atmospheric phenomena. They were also able to capture relatively high-quality photographs.

Unfortunately, both projects stalled because of insufficient funding. The Hessdalen research, however, was eventually followed up by that of a joint Italian–Norwegian team. This collaboration became the EMBLA 2000 project.

The new millennium dawned with the establishment of the EMBLA research team, which set out to conduct further monitoring activities in the Hessdalen Valley. Its members travelled to the site in August 2000, with the aim of continuing the work carried out by Erling Strand and his colleagues more than sixteen years earlier. The EMBLA team was a joint venture between the Institute of Radio Astronomy, a specific department of the National Council of Research (CNR), in Bologna, Italy, and the previously mentioned Ostfold College of Engineering. Its scientific supervisor was Massimo Teodorani, a consultant of the CNR, who was joined by Stelio Montebugnoli, the director of the radio astronomy station in Medicina of CNR-Bologna. Montebugnoli acted as the project's technical director, and the team was also joined by CNR engineer Jader Monari and several other researchers.

The team used radio spectrum analysers, which were in constant operation for twenty-five days, and its members also took part in many scheduled sky-watching sessions. Once again, unusual radio signals were detected and the researchers observed many luminous atmospheric phenomena in the area throughout their three and a half weeks on-site.

Again, previously unknown or little understood natural phenomena were mooted as a possible cause for at least some of the anomalous signals picked up. On this occasion, however, unlike in 1984, some of the observed aerial phenomena could not be construed as being plasma-like. Instead, some of them seemed to show a *structured* morphology.

In early 2000 T. Roy Dutton completed a comprehensive analysis of the Hessdalen events of 1984. It transpired that, of the 117 observations made during those thirty-five days, no fewer than 103 occurred within the plus-or-minus twenty-minute qualifying limits for acceptable correlation with his theory's projected timings.

The EMBLA 2000 team's data also had some curious parallels with Dutton's theory. In particular, the team's two most striking visual observations had very precise correlations with the timings indicated by Dutton's time graph for the Hessdalen Valley.

In scientific endeavours, funding has often been an underlying problem. Neither of the Hessdalen projects was to be an exception to this. The EMBLA project, like its predecessor, used the best equipment it could afford, but in both cases the need for better optical equipment was apparent. This point was made by Éamonn Ansbro at the SPIE conference in California in January 2001, and again at the First European Workshop on Exo-biology, held at Frascati, Italy, in May 2001. He noted this lack of specialised imaging equipment and decided to pursue the specific development and construction of the equipment that was so urgently needed. The fruits of his labour came later in the 2000s, when his newest systems were to play a crucial role in tracking UAP. This work was – and still is – conducted as part of the ongoing research into unexplained aerial events by the European UFO Survey (EUS).

The EUS, quietly established in the late 1980s, adopted a slightly more public profile from 2004 onwards. Despite publicising its existence, though, its members have otherwise firmly maintained a policy of anonymity, with Ansbro being a rare – even solitary – exception to that unwritten rule.

The group is made up of approximately thirty scientists from more than ten European Union countries and its members include computer specialists, astronomers, mathematicians, optical engineers, archaeologists, linguists and free energy researchers. Allied to these are certain UAP investigators from around the EU, with the overall thrust of the organisation's ethos veering away from the tired old arguments over whether non-earthly aerial vehicles exist and much more towards what it regards as a *fact* that aerial devices and/or craft from somewhere other than our own world do indeed pass through our airspace. The importance of this point is presented as a central tenet of the EUS mission statement, which says, in part, that 'ufology is fundamental for the present and future' of our planet. To the EUS, the otherworldly origin of some of these objects is a given, and it is time for science – and for the rest of humanity – to get on with deciding what comes next.[12]

The reluctance of the thirty or so members of the EUS group to go public is quite understandable. They come from the conservative worlds of industry and academia, where a career can be destroyed by daring to stick one's head above the parapet of 'acceptability' among professional peers. The EUS members, like many others around the world who have studied this subject, are all very familiar with the case of Harvard Medical School's John Mack. The late professor of psychiatry almost lost his career when he dared to study a taboo subject: reported cases of alleged alien abduction. Only after a protracted struggle did Mack prevail ... but it is anyone's guess how much the stress of his situation affected him personally.

Such caution has manifested very noticeably at times in how various unknown aerial phenomena are sometimes described in the EUS literature. A luminous object (or apparent object) becomes an ALP, meaning an Anomalous Light Phenomenon, while a more 'conventional' or 'nuts and bolts' one can be an AOP, an Anomalous Observational Phenomenon. The group's purpose is to describe what has actually been observed or recorded as accurately as possible and to steer towards a scientific angle – in other words, once and for all to veer away from hopelessly outdated, simplistic, overused and often ridiculed terms that have been propagated for decades by a poorly informed media. This includes such general one-size-fits-all terms as 'flying saucer', for example, an old chestnut coined by the US media in the late 1940s. (The predominant use of 'UAP' in this book reflects the fact that bizarre goings-on in our skies consist of a lot more than just unidentified *objects* being encountered. The 'Phenomena' part of the acronym includes the strange atmospheric – or even temporal – events that have been outlined in several of the cases discussed in earlier chapters.)

Other terms have also appeared in the verbal gymnastics in which air traffic controllers routinely engage to describe something odd being seen by pilots or themselves in the sky, or tracked on radar systems. This way, the controllers can also report to their superiors what members of the public might simply call a 'UFO', but their blushes can be spared by not having to use that acronym. The EUS, though, openly expresses its solid belief in the reality of such a phenomenon, while many (or perhaps most) air traffic controllers do not.

It remains to be seen what results the EUS comes up with, if it ever opts to make its findings more available to the general public, and any future link-ups with bodies such as the European Space Agency may prove very interesting. Certainly, it seems to be very well organised, with departments focused on physics, astrophysics, investigations, SETI, educational projects and media and international relations in place.[13]

One of the objectives of the EUS has been the design and use of advanced camera technology to capture detailed footage of unknowns in the sky. To this end it asked Kingsland Imaging Systems to develop a new camera system that could track airborne objects and take better quality images, yet which would cost no more than €3,000 per unit. This was a very challenging task, but by 2007 Éamonn Ansbro had provided just such a piece of equipment to the team.

On 10 February of that year, he liaised with EUS personnel in field testing his new camera system in Brittany, France. The range of tests was conducted in the area of Brest, which had been the location of a considerable amount of strange aerial activity – and which was also the home of a major French naval facility.

To put the new tracking system through its paces, clusters of helium-filled balloons were released during an eight-hour testing programme. In blustery weather conditions, the balloons moved in a fast, erratic manner, similar to the reported manoeuvres of some reported UAP. The system focused in on them successfully and recorded good quality, high resolution images at long distances. At 6.30 p.m. on 11 February, an unknown object appeared in mid-air, in full view of the team. The new system had not yet been set up, but other EUS cameras successfully filmed the item.

On 21 April of the same year, further tests were carried out by the EUS in Vence, near Nice in southern France. At this location, the team went up to a height of 3,937 feet (1,200 metres) in a mountainous area where there had been reported UAP sightings. Helium balloons were again released, and these were tracked and filmed by both the Discovery 1 (visible light) camera and the newer IR 1, which operates in the near-infrared band of the spectrum. Again, very good quality images were obtained using both pieces of equipment.[14]

FROM PERSONAL CURIOSITY TO A GLOBAL PHENOMENON

Everybody has their own opinion on whether any strange aerial phenomena are truly manifestations of visitations to our world by some non-human intelligence. With his interest in the realm of remote viewing, and his belief that consciousness is intrinsically linked to the nature of at least some UAP, Éamonn Ansbro has been more outspoken than many. Little did he know, when he was initially asked to look into some strange reports in the Irish south-west in the early 1990s, how widespread the phenomenon would prove to be. What began as a local project for him has since mushroomed to become an important global issue.

He is not alone in his opinion that consciousness and the power of the mind are important in all of this. For example, former Apollo 14 astronaut Edgar Mitchell was pivotal in establishing the Institute of Noetic Sciences in order to explore the frontiers of human consciousness. Also, American researcher Dr Steven Greer employed visualisation techniques as a component within his Disclosure Project, which led ultimately to dozens of former military, industry and intelligence people coming forward to tell publicly of what they had come across, during their careers, in relation to visitors coming to our world.

It has been Ansbro's contention that the key to success in the endeavour to contact extraterrestrial intelligence does not lie in the hope that ETs just happen to be listening in to radio signals from Earth and that they are then able (or willing) to respond. Rather, it lies in 'a combination of both science and the experiential' aspects of research. Furthermore, Ansbro has also stated the following, regarding how 'common sense' can sometimes come up short in explaining away all UAP in prosaic terms:

Common sense is not enough to understand unidentified aerial objects (or any other scientific anomaly). Those who argue that they are obviously nonsense and should be dismissed either do not understand the purpose of science or are being duplicitous. In order to make progress, science must examine scientific anomalies because they provide essential clues to the inadequacies of the existing theories.[15]

The efforts of this determined astronomer and the EUS in the field of remote viewing have provided the bare bones for a body of evidence. Designing and then deploying the advanced tracking and imaging systems to record these phenomena for further analysis is putting flesh on to those bones. This, surely, is what science is *supposed* to be about.

THE WATCHERS

Are any of the observed airborne oddities of non-terrestrial origin? The EUS maintains that 'yes' is the straightforward answer. If there is nothing to it, then it seems strange that contacts have been made with the EUS, ostensibly by American and British government representatives, asking the group to consider co-operating. These approaches, which the authors have known about since late 2005, were firmly rejected.

One must also wonder about the shadowing of a certain EUS member. With a background in a senior position within their country's intelligence community and living on mainland Europe, they routinely observed a car with two occupants parked close to their home, day and night. An overactive imagination at work? Paranoia? If so, then it hardly explains an unwelcome intrusion into Éamonn Ansbro's rural home while he was out of the country. In an incident reminiscent of the intrusion at Paul Redmond's home while he was researching the 1968 Tuskar Rock disaster off Ireland's south-eastern coast, nothing was stolen. Just like Redmond's case, however, only Ansbro's research materials had been interfered with.

Why, if his investigations and technical developments were of no official concern, was *someone* interested enough to break in and evaluate the extent of his research? It would appear that somebody 'in the know' about his activities, and who knew when the house would be vacant, was eager to take the opportunity to learn more about what he was working on. Who they were we may never know, but they seemed to have originated from the shadows of officialdom. Not Irish officialdom necessarily, but officialdom none the less. Such officialdom – as we shall see in this book's final pages – continues to block the efforts of researchers as they continue to probe the UAP realm.

For many years the authors, and many other researchers around the world, have continuously been in contact with military establishments and government agencies to secure information regarding unidentified aerial phenomena. Time after time, we were informed that they kept no files about, and had no interest in, this subject. Yet, in the past few years, several countries including France, the UK, Canada, Mexico, Sweden, Denmark, Uruguay and New Zealand have released previously classified documents focusing on UAP. Brazil, meanwhile, has recently released *thousands* of previously secret files which prove that, for many years, the country's government has been collating data from both civilian and military sources.

What other methods, one might wonder, will the authorities use to hinder researchers in their endeavours to uncover data, some of which may not be released for thirty years, fifty years – if ever?

FINAL THOUGHTS

In previous chapters, mysterious intrusions into the homes of two researchers have been discussed. With the 'burglars' showing interest solely in the researchers' work concerning unexplained aerial phenomena, there can surely be no doubt that the hand of officialdom was at work in both of these events. The perpetration of these acts constituted an erosion of the personal freedoms of both Paul Redmond and Éamonn Ansbro.

Such an erosion of personal freedom, undoubtedly designed to undermine one investigator's efforts, was intimated to the late Betty Meyler of the UFOSI group, as she explained while being interviewed with Carl Nally on Irish television in 2010. As she conducted research into the alleged 1996 crash of an unknown airborne object near her home in Boyle, County Roscommon, she was instructed by a local police officer – whose name and rank are in our file on the case – to stay away from probing into that incident in particular.[1]

Two members of the UFO Monitors East Kent (UFOMEK) group in the UK, Chris Rolfe and Jerry Anderson, experienced official interference as they investigated a triangular UAP over the home of the UK's Home

Secretary, Michael Howard, on 8 March 1997. Anderson called in a British Telecom technician to investigate his concern that his telephone had been tampered with. The technician found that someone had attempted, twenty times, to obtain his PIN to listen in to his messages. During the UFOMEK investigation, Anderson and Rolfe each received a cassette tape in the post, anonymously, which contained a telephone conversation they'd had about the incident. The conversation had taken place a year earlier, indicating that their research activities had been monitored for at least twelve months.[2]

In trying to sidestep the issue of the Flying Triangles (FTs) and their origin(s), some sceptical parties have pointed out that military developments of triangular (and circular) designs by Germany during the Second World War could have been further developed by the victorious Allies. The problem is that 'FT' reports have been discovered in American newspapers of the 1930s – years before the war, and an ocean away from Germany. Polish army troops at the coastal town of Kolobrzeg witnessed one emerging from the sea before darting away at speed into the sky. This incident, described by astronomer Jacques Vallée in his 1965 book, *Anatomy of a Phenomenon*, occurred in 1959. The Polish troops either saw otherworldly technology in action, or we must all wonder just how on earth Germany managed to lose the war.

Critics of the UAP phenomenon ask how the truth could be kept from the public. The answer is that it can, and has been repeatedly. The Manhattan Project, the development of the atomic bomb, ran from 1942 to 1945. It involved numerous installations across the US, cost the then colossal sum of more than two billion dollars and more than 50,000 people were involved. But no information about it ever leaked out until Hiroshima was attacked.[3] A test detonation in New Mexico on 16 July 1945 raised questions – until a compliant media published the 'truth', that it was merely an explosion at an ammunition dump.

To see how the media can be manipulated to feed disinformation to the public, one needs only to look at the events of 16 March 1967. On that day Robert Salas, a USAF first lieutenant at Malmstrom AFB, Montana, was underground in the Oscar Flight launch control centre for the base's Minuteman missiles. It was reported to him that a silent, red, circular object was hovering outside the base's main gate. Alarmingly, his missiles began to go off-line and thus could not be launched. A call came in from Echo Flight, 10 miles (16 km) away, informing him that it too had just experienced a parallel sighting of a similar object. In the case of Echo Flight, all of its missiles were inexplicably shut down. In *The Missing Times: News Media Complicity in the UFO Cover-up*, journalist Terry Hansen stated that eleven days later, on 27 March, the *Great Falls Tribune* finally mentioned the sightings, but it said that officials at Malmstrom AFB had stated that no unusual activity had been observed on radar and that no objects except aircraft were tracked.[4]

Under the Freedom of Information Act, Salas later

received a copy of a telegram which had been sent from the 15th Air Force headquarters to The Boeing Company, asking for assistance in evaluating what had occurred. The missiles were independently controlled, so a generic software problem could not have been the cause. When Dermot Butler spoke with Salas in 2008, the retired officer said that other episodes involving similar objects over US nuclear bases had also occurred. The most alarming of these happened on the night of 24–25 August 1966, when unidentified flying objects were observed for three and a half hours over Minuteman intercontinental ballistic missile (ICBM) silos at Minot AFB in North Dakota.[5]

The United States was not alone when it came to problems with these phenomena interfering with nuclear missile sites. In *Need To Know: UFOs, The Military and Intelligence* (2008), Timothy Good refers to a disturbing incident in which unidentified airborne objects hovered over a nuclear missile base in the Ukraine on 4 October 1982. Their presence led to unexplained interference with the missiles' launch codes and put the world on the brink of a nuclear war.

The denial of access to pertinent information regarding unexplained aerial phenomena was challenged in an American courtroom in the late 1970s by the Citizens Against UFO Secrecy (CAUS) organisation. The legal action involved the National Security Agency (NSA). CAUS had asked the CIA to conduct a search for any material it had on UFOs. Nuclear physicist and seasoned UFO researcher Stanton Friedman, in his excellent book, *Top Secret/Majic*, reported that the CIA produced nearly 900 pages of information. It also supplied a listing of fifty-seven files that had come its way from other intelligence agencies. Eighteen had come from the NSA, against whom an FOI Act suit was subsequently filed. A court-ordered search was carried out by the NSA, and it located 239 documents, of which 160 had originated within the NSA itself.

The agency declined to make the files available. Even Gerhard Geshell, the federal judge presiding over the case, was not permitted to see them. The actual twenty-one-page justification given to the judge for not releasing the files, was itself classified Above Top Secret.

From 1984 Friedman engaged in a protracted campaign to prompt the CIA to release files. Almost three years later, the agency released some documents to him. These contained only generic information, in the form of newspaper clippings, from Eastern Europe – information which anyone in the Warsaw Pact would have seen as soon as they were published. Further documents were withheld from him due to national security considerations. Finally, in 1989, the CIA contacted him to say that further documents he had sought were being withheld, again for national security reasons.[6]

The sky above us is a strange place. Whether it is encounters with unidentified flying objects, time distortions or spatial displacements, the domain of unidentified aerial pheno-smena is a place of enduring mysteries. The aviators who experience strange and even troubling events can only speculate on how and why they occur. Governments can and do supply disinformation to the media and to the public at large concerning these paranormal events. The Tuskar Rock incident, and the other cases discussed, may never be fully explained, but one can reasonably deduce that there was a lot more to these events than was officially acknowledged. As far as the reality of unexplained objects and other phenomena in our skies is concerned, the truth remains obscured in states of denial.

If any of our readers have experienced UAP or any other paranormal incidents, we would be grateful if they would contact us at upri98@gmail.com.

www.upri.uphero.com

NOTES

1 The Short Arm of the Law

1. *The Irish Sun*, 20 June 2008.
2. *Ibid.*
3. *The Times of India*, 21 June 2008.
4. Letter to headquarters, South Wales Police, 1 July 2008.
5. E-mail from Judith Hammett, South Wales Police, 10 July 2008.
6. Letter from David Wilson, director of contracts, Bond Air Services, 29 January 2009.
7. *Birmingham Mail*, 21 November 2008.
8. *Great Barr Observer*, 28 November 2008.
9. United Press International.
10. Interview with aviation contact, 22 August 2006.
11. Written statement from aviation contact, 24 August 2006.
12. *Fingal Independent*, 27 February 2004.
13. Letter to Garda Air Support Unit, 12 February 2007.
14. Letter to Garda Headquarters, 29 April 2007; letter to Irish Air Corps, 29 April 2007.
15. Undated letter from Sgt Donal Doyle, Garda Air Support Unit, May 2007.
16. Letter from Commandant E. Murphy, press officer, Irish Air Corps, 21 May 2007.
17. Letter from Ger Hegarty, divisional controller, MRCC, Irish Coast Guard, 18 July 2007.

2 Beams

1. *UFO DATA*, May-June 2008.
2. *Irish Daily Star*, 26 September 2008.

3. *The Irish Sun*, 27 September 2008.
4. *Irish Daily Star*, 29 September 2008; *Irish Independent*, 29 September 2008.
5. *Sunday World*, 5 October 2008.
6. *Sunday Tribune*, 5 October 2008.
7. *The Sunday Times*, 12 October 2008.
8. *Irish Mail on Sunday*, 12 October 2008.
9. *The Sunday Times*, 19 October 2008.
10. Letter to garda station, Dunboyne, 7 January 2009; letter to garda station, Dunboyne, 8 March 2009.
11. Letters from Niall Brooks, Climatological Division, Met Éireann, 8 January 2009 and 9 April 2009.
12. Letters from Graham Meates to IAA, 4 November 2008 and 2 January 2009.
13. Telephone call from Dunboyne garda station, 31 March 2009.
14. Letter from Tony Harkin, IAA, 13 May 2009.
15. E-mail from Valerie Young to UFO researchers, 15 October 2008.
16. Letter from Noel Dempsey, Irish Minister for Transport, 17 June 2009.
17. Letter to Rolls Royce, 17 July 2009; Letter to Safety Regulation Group, CAA, 17 July 2009.
18. *Irish Daily Mail*, 15 July 2009; *Metro*, 15 July 2009.
19. www.dailywhat.org.uk: accessed 4 February 2011.
20. www.manchesterairport.co.uk: accessed 4 February 2011.
21. *Daily Telegraph*, 25 March 2009.
22. Interviews with Karolina Dudek, September 2008 and October 2009.
23. Interview with Keith Mooney, 27 August 2009.
24. *Meath Weekender*, 19 August 2008.
25. *Ibid.*
26. Interview with George Rock, 11 August 2008.
27. Witness account and supplied image, 30 July 2008.
28. Interview with the Dolans, November 2008; completed witness

form, November 2008; correspondence with Dolans, March–April 2009.

29. Interview with witness, 26 February 2011.
30. *The Sun*, 6 November 2008; *The Irish Sun*, 6 November 2008.
31. *The Sun*, 10 November 2008.
32. Statement by Larry Warren, 9 May 2001.
33. Timothy Good, *Beyond Top Secret* (Sidgwick & Jackson, London, 1996).

3 Mystery at Tuskar Rock

1. Dermot Walsh, *Tragedy at Tuskar Rock* (Mercier Press, Cork, 1983).

4 Tuskar Rock – Case Unsolved

1. *The Sunday Times*, 10 January 1999.
2. *Irish Sunday Mirror*, 25 March 2007.
3. *Irish Mail on Sunday*, 16 September 2007.
4. Michael O'Toole, *Cleared for Disaster* (Mercier Press, Cork, 2006).
5. *Ibid.*
6. *Ibid.*
7. *Ibid.*
8. Walsh (1983).
9. *Ibid.*
10. *Ibid.*
11. *News of the World*, 8 June 2003.
12. Pat Kenny 'Today' page, www.rte.ie, accessed 28 February 2008.
13. *AFU Newsletter*, no. 37, July-August 1994.
14. *Ibid.*
15. Good (1996).
16. *Ibid.*
17. Dermot Butler and Carl Nally, *Conspiracy of Silence* (Mercier Press, Cork, 2006).

18. *Ibid.*
19. Timothy Good, *Unearthly Disclosure* (Century, London, 2000).
20. Interview with Timothy Good and Graham Sheppard, November 2004.

5   Strange Skies

1. Jay Gourley, *The Great Lakes Triangle* (Fontana, London, 1977).
2. *Ibid.*
3. *Ibid.*
4. *Ibid.*
5. *Ibid.*
6. Websites of the NTSB and FAA.
7. Martin Caidin, *Ghosts of the Air* (Bounty Books, London, 2005).
8. A. A. Quigley, *Green Is My Sky* (Avoca Publications, Dublin, 1983).
9. James Oberg, *Uncovering Soviet Disasters* (Random House, New York, 1988).
10. Information request to Canadian National Defence Headquarters, 2 August 2008.
11. Letter to FAA, 2 August 2008.
12. O'Toole (2006).
13. *Ibid.*
14. Telephone interview with Maureen O'Toole, 8 March 2008.

6   Science, Theory and UAP

1. *Roscommon Herald*, 13 July 2005.
2. 'Ireland's New Lord Rosse', *SPIN* magazine, Issue 11, 2005.
3. Patrick Moore, *Teach Yourself Astronomy* (Oldbourne, London, 1961).
4. 'Ireland's New Lord Rosse', *SPIN* magazine, Issue 11, 2005.
5. *Ibid.*

6. Butler and Nally (2006), pp. 117–26.
7. Mike Foylan, 'The Kingsland Observatory: New Horizons', *Astronomy & Space*, August 2006.
8. Éamonn Ansbro, 'New OSETI Observatory to Search for Interstellar Probes', paper Éamonn Ansbro, SPIE proceedings, vol. 4273, 2001.
9. *Ibid.*
10. *Ibid.*
11. UFO Roundup, vol. 7, no. 30; available at www.ufoinfo.com.
12. www.europeanufosurvey.com; accessed 16 February 2011.
13. *Ibid.*
14. É. Ansbro, 'Comparative Video Camera Imaging for UFO Research, A Report', 2007.
15. Éamonn Ansbro, *Beyond UFOs to Extra-terrestrial Intelligent Spacecraft in Our Vicinity* (published privately by É. Ansbro, 2005).

Final Thoughts

1. TV3 interview with Betty Meyler and Carl Nally, 28 January 2010.
2. *UFO Magazine*, January 2004, Quest Publications International Ltd.
3. Stanton Friedman, *Top Secret/Majic* (Marlow & Co., New York, 1996).
4. Terry Hansen, *The Missing Times: News Media Complicity in the UFO Cover-up* (Xlibris Corp., 2001).
5. Lecture by and interview with Robert Salas, Fifth Irish UFO Conference, 28 September 2008; Robert Salas and James Klotz, *Faded Giant* (BookSurge LLC, 2005).
6. Friedman (1996).

INDEX